Advance Praise for *We Are the Luckiest*

"*We Are the Luckiest* is a masterpiece. It's the truest, most generous, honest, and helpful sobriety memoir I've read. It's going to save lives."
— **Glennon Doyle,** #1 *New York Times* bestselling author of *Love Warrior*

"Laura McKowen's fearless, eloquent, powerful story is an ode to living an awakened life. Yes, this is a book about getting (and staying) sober, but it's so much more than that. It's about embracing the beautiful messiness of being human. Readers of *We Are the Luckiest* are lucky indeed."
— **Dani Shapiro,** *New York Times* bestselling author of *Inheritance: A Memoir of Genealogy, Paternity, and Love*

"Heartbreakingly candid and brave, Laura McKowen takes us on an unflinching journey of what it means to get sober. *We Are the Luckiest* explores what it means to reclaim one's life — and more. An unforgettable, soulful read."
— **Ann Dowsett Johnston,** author of *Drink: The Intimate Relationship Between Women and Alcohol*

"Vulnerability sounds great in theory and is hard as hell in practice. Laura McKowen writes with grace and wisdom — but also with huge vulnerability. By telling her story with raw, unflinching honesty, she invites us to look at our own stories with new compassion."
— **Claire Dederer,** bestselling author of *Poser: My Life in Twenty-Three Yoga Poses* and *Love and Trouble: A Midlife Reckoning*

"Laura speaks to that place within us where what breaks our heart becomes our highest learning and our most invaluable currency."
— **Elena Brower,** bestselling author of *Practice You*

"Laura McKowen is a stunning writer, and this book is a gift for everyone: the newly sober, those with longtime sobriety, those for whom the sands are beginning to shift, and those who simply aren't sure where they stand. This is beautiful, revelatory writing filled with grace and awareness about what it means to be a complicated human being living in a complicated world, and not only surviving, but thriving. It will be a blessing for everyone who reads it."

— **Elissa Altman,** author of
Motherland: A Memoir of Love, Loathing, and Longing

"In a voice both direct and kind, Laura McKowen shines a shame-erasing light on her history of addiction and illuminates the lucky life she found in its wake. Through personal stories and practical advice, she offers readers a path to the other side of their own struggles — and more importantly, she illustrates with eloquence and vividness why that path is more than worth the effort. As a person in long-term sobriety, even I found inspiration and useful tips in this warm, compassionate book."

— **Kristi Coulter,** author of *Nothing Good Can Come from This*

"*We Are the Luckiest* is a hope-inducing dose of narrative medicine for those who fear that life ends after drinking does. Like a long, honest conversation with a very good friend, Laura's story is a gift to anyone starting out on that scary, lucky path."

— **Melissa Febos,** author of *Whip Smart* and *Abandon Me*

"*We Are the Luckiest* is ultimately about the wild and holy effort of trying to face this great big unsayable love inside us without numbing ourselves from its blazing truth or distancing ourselves from the fact that it's here with us, whether we ever believe we're worthy of it or not. Laura McKowen's words are drenched with proof of the existence of this unsayable love, and with hope that it's never too late for any of us to begin to say *yes* to a life that's courageously present to it."

— **Meggan Watterson,** *Wall Street Journal* bestselling author of
Mary Magdalene Revealed

We Are the Luckiest

The Surprising Magic of a Sober Life

LAURA McKOWEN

New World Library
Novato, California

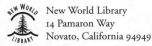 New World Library
14 Pamaron Way
Novato, California 94949

Permission acknowledgments on page 231 are an extension of the copyright page.

The material in this book is intended for education. It is not meant to take the place of diagnosis and treatment by a qualified medical practitioner or therapist. No expressed or implied guarantee of the effects of the use of the recommendations can be given or liability taken.

Some names and identifying characteristics have been changed.

Text design by Tona Pearce Myers

Library of Congress Cataloging-in-Publication Data

Names: McKowen, Laura, date, author.
Title: We are the luckiest : the surprising magic of a sober life / Laura McKowen.
Description: Novato, California : New World Library, [2020] | Summary: "A memoir of
    alcohol addiction and recovery, written by a successful career woman who describes
    the joys and challenges of staying sober in a culture permeated by drinking."
    --Provided by publisher.
Identifiers: LCCN 2019042319 (print) | LCCN 2019042320 (ebook) | ISBN 9781608686544
    (hardback) | ISBN 9781608686551 (epub)
Subjects: LCSH: McKowen, Laura, date- | Recovering alcoholics--United States--Biography. |
    Alcoholics--Rehabilitation--United States.
Classification: LCC HV5293.M35 A3 2020 (print) | LCC HV5293.M35 (ebook) | DDC
    362.292092 [B]--dc23
LC record available at https://lccn.loc.gov/2019042319
LC ebook record available at https://lccn.loc.gov/2019042320

First printing, January 2020
ISBN 978-1-60868-654-4
Ebook ISBN 978-1-60868-655-1
Printed in Canada on 100% postconsumer-waste recycled paper

 New World Library is proud to be a Gold Certified Environmentally Responsible Publisher. Publisher certification awarded by Green Press Initiative.

10   9   8   7   6   5   4   3   2   1

For Alma

1. It is not your fault.
2. It is your responsibility.
3. It is unfair that this is your thing.
4. This is your thing.
5. This will never stop being your thing until you face it.
6. You cannot do it alone.
7. Only you can do it.
8. I love you.
9. I will never stop reminding you of these things.

Contents

Introduction   1

1. This Is My Thing   9
2. Forget Forever   19
3. Stop Getting on the Train   33
4. Find a House Where the Truth Is Told   51
5. Push Off from Here   67
6. Hell Is Other People   79
7. The Pregnancy Principle   103
8. Fantasy Island   119
9. A Bigger Yes   141
10. The Truth about Lying   153
11. Burning Lonely   181
12. We Are All Magnificent Monsters   193
13. The Wrong Damn Question   201
14. A Nice Little Life   209

Acknowledgments   227
Permission Acknowledgments   231
About the Author   233

Introduction

"How did you go bankrupt?" Bill asked.
"Two ways," Mike said. "Gradually and then suddenly."

— ERNEST HEMINGWAY, *The Sun Also Rises*

On July 13, 2013, the night of my brother's wedding, I left my four-year-old daughter alone in a hotel room overnight because I was blackout drunk. It shouldn't have been a surprise, but it was — to me, to my family, to my friends who found out later. I had a twenty-year history with alcohol and sometimes it looked problematic, but mostly — except for the last couple of years, and even then only if you got *really* close — things looked normal enough. I was a thirty-five-year-old director at a global marketing agency, a marathon runner, a yoga teacher, and a mama to one. I rented a sweet home in an affluent seaside town north of Boston, I had plenty of friends and family who loved me and wanted me around, and although my marriage had recently fallen apart, I was ostensibly doing quite all right.

Except I wasn't. I was so far from all right.

That night, the two worlds I'd been trying so diligently to keep separate collided: my interior life, full of secrets and cover-ups, nightly blackouts with wine and Ambien, crushing anxiety and exhaustion, and a growing fear of myself; and the external one, where I hosted dinner parties and brought my daughter to playdates, got better jobs and more promotions, dressed well, and regularly ran six miles around Boston at lunch. Waking up in a hotel room and realizing it was not *my* hotel room, that the body next to me wasn't the sweet-smelling anchor of my baby girl but instead a strange man's — a guest of the wedding, as I recalled — was nuclear. Just impossible. Despite all the trouble my drinking had brought me, I truly didn't think it could ever supplant my mama instinct, my internal homing device that had always led me back to her, even in the dark, even when I was unconscious.

The next morning on my brother's porch in Colorado, he recounted for me what had happened. I winced and gasped and choked on tears, and then he gently but firmly spoke the words I most dreaded hearing. "Laura. You aren't someone who can drink. Other people can, but not you. You just can't."

I knew he was right. Somewhere inside — maybe since I was eighteen — I'd known this conversation was imminent. And yet I'd still managed to convince myself it couldn't happen — not to me, not to *someone like me*. Over the coming days, weeks, and months, I'd beg for something else. *Anything — give me anything else.*

I know you're probably thinking that's when the tide turned, right? I left my daughter in a goddamn hotel room, and she could have been stolen, taken from me, or any number of other horrific scenarios could have played out. I imagine you're assuming this was the proverbial "rock bottom" you've heard about, after which I surrendered, got myself into a 12-step program, and reluctantly but gratefully built a new life in sobriety.

Right?

Yeah, I thought it would be, too — or at least I thought it most certainly *should* be. While that night put a pin in my drinking and pricked a large hole in the bubble of my denial, it wasn't the end. In some ways it was really only the beginning.

For the next year, I found out what hell on earth really was.

I wouldn't — couldn't — didn't — get sober for more than another year. And in that time, I was burned to ash over and over and over again. I totaled my car. I woke up with more strangers. I put my daughter in danger. I fell so far out of integrity with myself, I didn't trust I'd ever return. Not really. All the qualities that had served me so well up to that point — my willpower, charm, optimism, determination — couldn't carry me through this, not all the way. I didn't know what would.

And yet, in that time, I also started to taste a life without the stranglehold of drinking and its consequences. Eventually I made it through my first sober weekend in fifteen years, save the nine months of my pregnancy. I had my first sober Thanksgiving. Christmas. New Year's Eve. I went to a sober Fourth of July barbecue and spent all twenty-four hours of my thirty-sixth birthday unpunctuated with wine. I started to meet a few sober people. I experienced the relief of mornings without a hangover or regret.

I put together days, then a couple of weeks here and there. I started to really kill it at work and even got promoted to vice president. I walked through big and small moments of my life sans alcohol. And although sometimes only by a thread, and although I often wanted to scream at the discomfort and unfairness of it all, and although I often wanted to rip off my skin, I slowly started to familiarize myself with the terrain of this new landscape.

Sobriety began to sing to me in a foreign but nostalgic tongue, like a language I maybe once knew but forgot. You see, I had always been a seeker. From the time I was young, I had a thirst for the deeper answers. *Who were we? What were we doing here? What did we really want? What is God?* My first sources of study were books — anything I could get my hands on — and music, and eavesdropping on adult conversations when I wasn't allowed to just sit there and listen. By my thirties I'd read every spiritual and self-help book out there, and once iPods were invented, I constantly had teachers like Pema Chödrön, Wayne Dyer, Caroline Myss, and Marianne Williamson piping through my ears. As I started to experience sobriety, a recognition grew inside me. All I had absorbed over the years — the spiritual teachings, the questions of existence and suffering and meaning — they were no longer ideas I could passively explore; I had to test them against my own experience. I had to actually live into answering them, for myself.

Also from a very young age, I felt this presence in me. I used to call it a "big energy." It fueled me to read and draw and craft and create whatever I could. It made me spontaneously cry when I heard someone sing from their soul; when I'd listen to live music; or when I'd see an athlete, a dancer, or anyone perform in their element.

Later, in my twenties and thirties, when I felt the big energy bubble up in my chest and I found myself in the company of the right kind of friend, I'd ask, "Do you ever feel like...I don't know...you have something really big inside of you? Something that wants to be born?" A few friends nodded knowingly, asking what I thought my thing was. Once or twice I confessed, "I think it's writing. I want to write." But usually that felt too ridiculous, so I'd just shrug and let the question fade into the background again.

When I started to get sober, the big energy burst forth like a tidal wave. It was as if everything I'd been tamping down with alcohol crashed forward, and I began to write as if possessed. My mind was spinning constantly with ideas. I had no idea how to speak the truth in my real life, so I began to type it into screens first. I created a new Instagram account called @clear_eyes_full_hearts and started to post little bits of my experience. For a lover of words and images, it was perfect — I could post my favorite quotes and pictures and practice stringing together words to describe what was really going on with me. I dusted off my blog and started writing there, too. For the very first time in my life, at the age of thirty-seven, I started telling the truth.

It helped. I connected with other people who were in the same place. I found that even in my limited experience with sobriety, I had something to offer, as if there was a part of me that recognized this place I was heading already — that I had inhabited it before. I had a sense that sobriety — as much as it felt like a death sentence, like the unluckiest turn of fate — might hold some secrets I'd been longing to hear my whole life. This feeling would come and go. As incensed as I sometimes felt, more often I was wading in loneliness and anger and grief. I wrote about that, too. I wrote about everything.

One morning toward the end of my drinking, I emerged from a steamy underground train station in Boston on my way to work. I was terribly hungover again, shaking, sweaty, and brimming with rage — at myself, but more at this thing that still had me by the throat. I wondered: *Where are my people, and why aren't we talking about this?*

I didn't mean, *Where are the alcoholics in quiet rooms talking about alcoholism?* I'd been to hundreds of meetings and found invaluable help and comfort there. I didn't mean, *Where are the memoirs documenting train-wreck stories of addiction and eventual recovery?* I'd read all those books twice.

I meant, Why aren't we — the collective we, as in you and me — talking about this *out loud*? Why — if we really want people to feel unashamed, and society to shift its misunderstandings and perceptions of addiction — do we still insist on anonymity and speaking in hushed, unfortunate tones? I didn't quite buy that the only people who were in trouble with drinking were the ones qualified to be in a 12-step meeting, and I didn't buy that all my deepest "character flaws" were unique to me as an "alcoholic." Drinking did something different to me than some people, yes, but *everyone* I knew was running, numbing, escaping from themselves and their lives somehow.

Something big was amiss. This was bigger than alcohol, or addiction.

There was hiding and denying, everywhere.

Why did we try so hard not to see this? Why were we so afraid to tell the truth?

September 28, 2014, was my last Day One. I didn't know it would be at the time. In fact, the only promise I made to myself that morning was that I wouldn't make any more promises to myself.

As I write this today, it is now almost five years later, and in that time I've poured everything I have into answering those questions. This book is what I know of the answers — for me, for you, for all of us.

Maybe you didn't get addicted to drinking booze, or taking pills, or trying to go unconscious night after night. Maybe your thing is chasing love, or sex, or being perfect, or keeping your body very small. Maybe you don't have a thing, but you still feel a deadness inside and there's a voice that haunts you — it finds you every morning just after you wake, before you remember yourself — whispering, *Listen to me. Say yes to me.*

I finally did it — I said yes. This book is the story of how, and what happened next. And I'm telling you the story I share in the pages that follow because I hope you'll say yes, too. To yourself. To the voice. To all the terror and magic that follow. It is worth it. I could promise, but I won't. Instead, how about you see for yourself?

1

This Is My Thing

Do you know why this cup is useful?
Because it is empty.

— BRUCE LEE

It was September 2014, and I was sitting alone in my car. It was late Saturday night and cold enough that I could see my breath, which was sending small billowing clouds of moisture into the air. I closed my eyes and focused on the breathing. *In and out. In and out.* Again and again.

From inside my car, I watched as my brother stepped out of the restaurant and stood under the streetlights looking around, reaching into his pocket for his phone. I turned off the car and jumped out.

"Joe!" I yelled across the parking lot.

He couldn't see me, but he heard my voice, and when he did, his expression shifted from worried to angry. *Fuck.* I exhaled and started toward him, wiping my eyes.

"We were looking for you, Laura," he said, when I reached the sidewalk.

We were throwing a surprise party for our mom's sixtieth birthday. Joe and his wife, Jenny, had flown in the day before, along with a few of my mom's closest friends and family members. Over fifty people were gathered inside an old Italian restaurant — not unlike the one we'd owned back in Colorado when we were growing up. Everyone was inside drinking, eating, and dancing. Around nine o'clock, once the party was really underway, I snuck out to my car to breathe, or cry, or do anything, really, to release the vise grip of anxiety that had been crushing me since I woke up hungover that morning.

"I'm here," I said, apologetically. "I had to breathe."

I could barely look at him. I knew he was worried I'd gone off to drink. I wanted to tell him not to worry. I was a thirty-seven-year-old grown-ass adult. A mother! His big sister! Someone who managed million-dollar budgets! And a whole team! But I couldn't say any of that, because just yesterday, minutes after I picked them up at the airport, I'd stuck them with my daughter, Alma, while I went off to "run errands," which looked like me wandering around my town drinking nips of cheap cherry vodka and warm white wine from my purse all afternoon, then laughably trying to hide the fact that I was blasted when we met back at my place. As if he wasn't my brother, as if he wouldn't know just by looking at me.

All day, blurry scenes from the night had been torturing me: Me trying to get Alma dressed back at my house so we could go surprise my mom at a restaurant with Joe and Jenny's arrival; Joe driving us to the restaurant in my car while I sat in the back with Alma, like a child; us arriving at the restaurant and my mom's initial joy upon seeing them, followed by her falling expression when she turned to me and noticed I was not sober; my mom following me into the restaurant bathroom, where I kept going to try to sneak sips of wine from the water bottle in my purse; later, my brother back at home, ushering me to bed. Alma, poor Alma, during all of this. It was a dance I knew too well: The humiliating scenes from the night before replaying on loop. The swollen lump of terror pulsing in my throat. The panic. The acidic shame. And above all, my weary, broken heart.

I just couldn't *believe* I'd done it…again. I hadn't even seen it coming.

"I thought you were doing better," Joe had said earlier that morning, sipping his coffee, sitting in my living room. It was both a statement and a question. He lived two thousand miles away. We talked somewhat regularly, but just like everyone else, he only knew what I chose to tell him. I hadn't told anyone the full truth: that despite spending far more days sober than not in the past year, I still found myself drinking quite a lot, and almost always alone; that I hated everything about drinking by then but still didn't know how to let it go completely; that it made no sense — there was no good reason why or logic to it any longer; that I was terrified, I was angry, and I was so lonely that sometimes my teeth hurt.

It was at his wedding the summer before that I'd left Alma in the hotel room alone. It was he who had to answer a phone call on my behalf the next morning. And it was he who sat with me the following day on his porch and told me kindly, but in no uncertain terms, that the show was over.

A whole year, and here we were again.

We stood facing each other in front of the restaurant, silent for a full minute.

"Yeah, well, your daughter is inside looking for you," he finally said. "There's a party going on, you know."

I noticed then that he was pretty buzzed, and I read in his posture, his expression, all the things he wasn't saying: *Tough shit. Get over yourself and get back into Mom's party. This isn't about you. I'm worried; I hate that I worry about you. Please be okay. I'm scared; I'm angry; I love you.*

"I'm sorry, Joe. I'm right here." I stared past him into the window at the party. The lights from the streetlamp bounced off the pools of tears in my eyes, blurring my vision. I wiped them and looked back at him.

"I'm sorry this is hard, sister," he said. And he meant it, I knew.

I shook my head. I couldn't handle his tenderness.

"It *is* hard, and I —" I stopped myself. I wanted to say I was sorry. Sorry I had ruined everything again by drinking on Friday and tainting what was supposed to be a great weekend for Mom, for all of us. Sorry that I was sometimes okay, but then other times, I just wasn't. Sorry that he had to worry about his big sister. Just...*sorry.* But he already knew all that. Saying those things would be a selfish attempt to off-load some of my self-loathing onto him.

A few tears fell straight to the ground.

Finally, I looked up at him. "I hate this. But it's mine."

I felt the weight of those words land between us. I had never said this before, not without follow-up of caveats, explanations, excuses, pleas for sympathy. "I know it's mine."

He nodded. "That's right, Laura. It's yours. This is your thing."

"Yeah," I replied. On the other side of the window, people milled around, lost in the party. An eruption of laughter boomed from the back patio where people were dancing. My mom spotted us and waved for us to come back in.

I knew drinking was going to be my thing long before the night of our mom's sixtieth birthday party, even if I refused to let that knowing arrive fully into my consciousness. I knew it in college when one of my guy friends, while retelling a story from a crazy party we'd been at the night before, joked that I probably wouldn't remember — *because I was always too drunk to remember* — and I felt like crawling into a hole and dying.

I knew it in my twenties, living in Boston, when my girlfriends continually joked about whose turn it was to take care of me, before we went out to the bars.

I knew it by the urgency I felt chugging champagne before my wedding, and I knew it later, after my husband and I learned I was pregnant. I drank the occasional glass here and there throughout my pregnancy — sometimes pushing the limit from one to one and a half glasses — but aside from the wine not feeling good physically, I realized how much I relied on it to soften my experience.

It was so incomplete to me, so unsatisfying, to have only one glass. To have a limit.

Often in those pregnant months, I'd be going about my day and suddenly be struck by an overwhelming urge to reach for wine. *Something* to take the edge off. And not being able to drink sent a surprising jolt of panic through me. Before my pregnancy, my drinking could at least be contextualized. I was having fun, going out after work, hanging out with the girls, Sunday Funday, "relaxing." But now that I couldn't have a drink anytime I wanted one, it was alarming how often I wanted one.

It was the first time it had scratched at my consciousness that perhaps drinking had morphed elusively into something I not only liked but also needed. If not physically, then certainly emotionally.

I'm not sure if you've ever *needed* something like this.

Maybe you top off your drink when nobody's looking, like I used to do. Maybe you're like my friend Brent and you eat McDonald's Big Macs and whole Domino's cheese pizzas in your car on the way home from work, before dinner. Maybe you can't leave a man who regularly beats the hell out of you, even though when he knocked you unconscious last week, you swore it was the last time. Maybe you're the one who's been slicing into your body with razor blades since you were sixteen, because the pain needs a place to go.

Maybe — *maybe* your thing is less severe or more socially acceptable, like staying at the office past your kids' bedtime most nights because work is the only place you feel in control, or maybe you wrestle with crippling perfectionism. Maybe it's the red-hot hatred you feel toward every woman pushing a stroller since you discovered you couldn't get pregnant last spring, or maybe you keep trying to untangle the knot of rage in your chest that *just never leaves*.

I don't know what your thing is, but alcohol was mine.

And here is the thing we must know about our things if we are ever going to survive them: We believe we can bury them, when the truth is, they're burying us. They will always bury us, eventually.

By the time I stood in that parking lot with Joe, I'd been trying to get sober for a year. And actually, *trying* is a generous word since it was only sometimes true. Most of the time I was just pretending to want a thing I did not want. At that point, sobriety for me meant no longer drinking. That's how most people think about it — abstinence from alcohol or drugs. But it actually has a much broader context. One of the definitions of sobriety is to be clearheaded. In that way, sobriety is about freeing yourself from any behavior, relationship, or way of thinking that enslaves you and keeps you from being present to life.

At recovery meetings I would say, "Hi, I'm Laura, and I'm an alcoholic," and in so many moments I said, "I am done" and "I give up." I meant every statement at the time — as much as you can mean a thing you don't know how to mean. But deep down I was still holding on to those last final threads of my own plan. I was still hoping for a third door: another option besides door number one (drinking) and door number two (sobriety). I simply could not fathom that there wasn't a fucking third door.

But there, standing in the parking lot with my brother, something new happened. Something I had not experienced before. Some kind of surrender beyond me. Less like I had let go of something and more like, after all my begging, it had let go of me. Who knows why it happened then. Perhaps it was the magical number of attempts; perhaps it was the look on my brother's face: a combination of pain, fear, and anger. But when I look back, I think it was the anxiety more than anything else — the jaw-breaking, soul-crushing anxiety that inevitably followed a night of drinking — it had been clobbering me all day.

For so long, I thought alcohol had helped me relieve anxiety — that's what it promises, right? But somewhere along the line, I realized the equation was actually reversed: drinking alcohol was like pouring gasoline on my anxiety. Maybe I'd feel some relief for a little while, but then — *boom* — I was spinning like a top. Each morning after was worse than the last.

That morning, Alma had had a soccer game. Joe and Jenny had wanted to come, and the plan had been for my mom and her husband, Derek, to meet us at the field. Alma's dad would be there, too. I had barely been able to push through the task of getting myself dressed, putting her uniform on her squirming five-year-old body, corralling her to the car, driving to the game, standing in the blazing sun next to all the other families, and trying to actually appear okay — *as if nothing had happened at all!* — while I was shaking, dizzy, and near choking on dread. I'd endured hundreds, if not thousands, of bad mornings, but this one felt like it might end me. I thought, *I can't do one more day like this. Not one. I'd rather die.*

This is what I can see now, but all I knew in that moment standing in front of the restaurant with my brother was this: This thing was mine. My responsibility.

Before that night I had been trying to tolerate sobriety like the flu or another long Boston winter — subconsciously believing that eventually it would end, and I'd return to normal. That night, I suppose, was the first time I realized that this was my normal. This was my life.

I wish I could say that was the end of the suffering. It wasn't. But it was the end of a certain kind of fight.

In *The Divine Comedy*, Dante described purgatory as a place where the soul is cleansed of all impurities. It is known as a place where suffering and misery are felt to be sharp, but temporary. This for me was what it felt like to have one foot in the new, strange land of sobriety and the other firmly, desperately, in my old life. This is what it feels like for all of us, I think, when we have only half-decided to own our thing. When we have only half-surrendered, only half-committed to becoming different.

We live in purgatory. The pain is sharp.

In my mind, as I stood there that night, waiting for Joe to say something — anything — to make the pain stop, I thought of Wile E. Coyote. I thought of that moment when the earthquake hits and the ground splits in two and that poor coyote is grasping, all wide-eyed and panicked, at both sides of the earth. The divide becomes bigger, bigger, bigger, and his body starts stretching like a rubber band until finally he's unable to keep any grip. Then, when he can't hold on any longer, he floats suspended in the air, holding on to nothing at all, before he plummets into the canyon, *crash*. A delayed plume of smoke.

I thought about how anything would be better than this. This purgatory. This unbearable wishing for one side or another. This unsustainable stretching. My inevitable crash landing. I was going to have to pick a side.

The same is true for all of us when it comes to our things. We have to pick a side. If we ever want out of purgatory, we have to decide if we are going back to a life of denial and secrecy and hiding and gripping onto the thing we do not know how to live without, or if we are going to take a stab at doing a thing we have never done before.

If you know your thing, that's good news, although I know it doesn't feel that way. It doesn't mean it's fair. It doesn't mean letting go and moving through will be easy. It doesn't mean you have any idea what the fuck to do next — I certainly didn't. It just means you're no longer willing or able to fight to keep it in your life.

That night, I returned to the party long enough to gather my tired little girl and say my goodbyes. I did not know what I was supposed to do next. No one does.

With Alma sleeping in the back seat, I opened the window to let the thick, warm coastal air fill the car as I played a song by My Morning Jacket called "The Bear" on repeat. The lyrics rang out and over and through me: "The time is near / to come forward with / whatever killed your spark."

2

Forget Forever

If fear is the absence of breath,
and faith is a positive force,
I want to breathe into an uncertain future.

— LAUREN E. OAKES, *In Search of the Canary Tree*

Monday morning after my mom's birthday-party weekend, I woke at four to my heart slamming against my rib cage. It took a moment to get my bearings. I went through a mental checklist I had done thousands of other times, although usually not sober.

It's Monday morning; I'm in my bed; Alma is next to me; I went to bed sober; nothing bad happened yesterday; Joe and Jenny are asleep in Alma's room.

For a second my heart settled.

My mind scrambled through the coming day's agenda: get Alma ready for preschool, drop Joe and Jenny off at Logan airport on my way to work, then prepare for the big pitch meeting

I was running later that afternoon. I reached up and touched my eyes, which were swollen from crying. My whole body was puffy and tight.

The truth is, I'd made it through the rest of the weekend just fine. Everyone — my brother, Jenny, my mom, Derek — had offered their own expressions of love and compassion after Friday's errand-running episode and we'd silently agreed that we would move on.

But here I was, lying in my bed on the morning of another Day Three, trying again to ward off the string of horrible thoughts and flashbacks of memory from Friday that kept battering my psyche. Pawning off Alma. Lying about what I was doing. Trying to pretend like I wasn't drunk later on. Stashing miniature bottles in my purse and around the house. Seeing Joe's frustration. Knowing I stained the whole weekend. It was all too much. My inner monologue started to rip at me.

How have we arrived here again? You're never going to do this, are you? You don't deserve to be a mother. You don't deserve her.

It was more than just the anxiety and self-criticism that was getting me. I felt empty, too. Like someone had gutted me. Scooped me out like a Halloween pumpkin.

I'd been here so many times. Too many times.

I rolled over to check my phone. No messages. No calls. By the glow of the streetlamp outside, I stared at the photo on my bedside table. The dim light illuminated Alma's four-month-old face in the picture frame — bald, save a little patch of fuzz peeking out from the back of her hairline. She bore the same porcelain skin and shocking blue eyes she has now. I stood holding her, squinting into the Colorado sun, looking peaceful and knowing, though I wasn't. My husband, her dad, had taken the picture.

Jake.

We'd been separated for more than two years now but had yet to file the divorce paperwork. I had the impulse to call him. It would be such comfort to hear his voice, for him to tell me I would be okay — that everything would be okay.

But we weren't those people to each other anymore. I couldn't call him at this hour, and it wasn't his job to tell me that.

Instinctively, I swiped my phone open to send some texts: to my friend Holly, to the man I'd been dating on and off, to sober people who would say the right things. I wanted to start building the case for myself again, to declare my new resolve, to announce my place again: Day Three. But I couldn't. I'd done that so many times.

Forever.

Forever.

That word was so hard for me.

The idea that I would give up drinking forever.

The words, Rumi's words, came to mind — as they had over the past year. The words are written on scraps of paper tucked in my wallet, my backpack, various coats, desk drawers, and journals. I'd whispered them to myself many mornings after drinking, or while riding the train in to work. I'd squeeze the words in the palm of my hand while quiet tears streamed down my face. I'd recite them as I brushed my teeth, looking into the mirror, asking myself, *Why, baby? Why again? When will enough be enough?*

I'd rolled them around in my head when I was lying in a hospital last winter, having just totaled my car, and it was just me and the machines and my blood still simmering with booze.

I used the words as a prayer, a promise, a mantra, a wish bigger than any other wish I'd cast up: to find it in me to stop; to want what I did not want; for God — or something, or someone — to love me while I kept trying, to let me keep coming back.

Lying there in my bed, I whispered them again to myself.

Come, come, whoever you are.
Wanderer, worshipper, lover of leaving.
It doesn't matter.
Ours is not a caravan of despair.
Come, even if you have broken your vows a thousand times.
Come, yet again, come, come.

Rumi's words. Rumi, who knew, so long ago.

I had broken my vows at least a thousand times. I found my thoughts threading familiar pathways: making plans, problem-solving, fighting to build solid ground.

I'll go to a meeting every day, no matter what, even though I hate them.

I'll call my sponsor every day.

I'll reset my sobriety-counter app in my phone and resolve to never, ever, ever change it again.

I'll cancel all my work trips.

I'll cancel any plans.

I'll bear down.

Do more. Do less.

Fix it.

But the wheels just wouldn't move. I couldn't get there. I was so damn tired. I focused on my breath instead. With each breath, I willed my heartbeat to slow down. I gently clasped Alma's hand, and I whispered the simplest, four-word prayer:

Please let me sleep.

One of the most counterintuitive things about sobriety, for me, has been how much effort it takes and how it takes no effort at all. How easy it is to try harder and how truly impossible it feels to not try at all. And how, when all is said and done, the "forever" we're so desperate to achieve is possible only through the quiet surrender of right now.

I woke up again to Joe standing in my doorway, sipping coffee. "We have to get going, sister."

I looked at the clock. Past seven thirty. "Shit. Yes, we do."

I raced through the routine of getting Alma and myself ready, and for a minute I was able to forget about all the drama. But then, as I was digging in my closet for a pair of shoes, something rolled out of a duffel bag and onto the closet floor, making a hollow *clunk-clunk-clunk* sound. My heart leaped into my throat, and I scrambled to stuff the bottle back into the bag, under some clothes. An empty wine bottle. Cheap white wine.

It flooded back: I hid it there Friday, thinking it would give me a safety stash for later, since I couldn't drink in front of Joe and Jenny; it was the wine I'd put in the water bottle in my purse when we went to the restaurant. I flashed back to when Jake and I were still together but approaching the end, and I used to toss mini bottles of wine out my car window when I pulled up at home after work. I'd often buy them on the commute home and drink one or two or sometimes all four from the four-pack before I made it home. If I hadn't disposed of them elsewhere on the ride, I'd fling them into the bushes next to the driveway as I pulled up, feeling a little thrill of defiance and power in my secrecy — a false bravado born of the alcohol. More than once, he had plucked one out from the bushes, asking me where the hell it came from, and I had shrugged.

How would I know? I don't drink that shit.

It's bizarre how well I could dissociate from my own

behavior, as if I actually believed I wasn't who was doing those things. For a split second when the bottle fell in the closet, I had the same indignant reaction. *Who the hell put that there?* I could not connect the person who hid alcohol in closets to who I imagined I was.

I pictured myself picking it up, smashing it against the wall, and howling. That would feel good. That would accurately represent how I felt about this thing that had broken my soul. Of course, I didn't. I made a mental note to throw it away when I got home that night.

We all climbed into the car together. First we dropped off Alma at preschool, and then on the way into the city with Joe and Jenny, I turned on Marc Maron's *WTF* podcast, the episode with Dax Shepard. I'd been listening to a lot of *WTF* in the past year. Maron himself is sober and interviews comedians, musicians, and the occasional Hollywood director or actor — many of whom are sober as well. Recovery is never the main point of the conversation, but, back then especially, it was comforting to hear mentions of it here and there, or a story of what the guest used to be like — because I got to hear them on the other side, where getting sober was now just a part of their bigger story, not the defining and all-consuming thing it was for me. Mostly, it felt good to hear them laugh. I desperately needed to laugh.

The conversation with Dax was particularly funny. I'd listened to it a few times by then, but I chose it that morning because they spend a decent amount of time talking about Dax's battle with drinking. I wanted Joe and Jenny to hear the jokes, and hopefully the earnestness in Dax's voice. It was my way of acknowledging what had happened without speaking about it directly, to apologize again, and to say, *See — this happens. And he's okay. I am trying. I will get this.*

After I dropped them off at the airport, I drove to the train-station parking lot where I boarded every day to go to work. I started down the steps toward the train but just couldn't bring myself to board yet. I was too rattled. I'd been holding on to so much since Friday night — trying to appear together. I had hoped I could prove to Joe and Jenny and everyone else that weekend that I was okay, and it was only now, really — now that they were gone — that I realized how hard that had been to carry. So instead of going down the stairs, I turned and followed the steps up to the top of the garage. I'd never gone all the way up before. But I stepped out at the rooftop level and sucked in deep breaths of air as I marveled at the 360-degree view of the city.

I pulled out my phone and dialed Jake.

Jake and I met in my late twenties at a Memorial Day party at a mutual friends' house on Cape Cod. It was a misty, uncharacteristically cold day, and my friend Heather and I were huddled inside the living room having screwdrivers when I saw him tossing around a football outside with a group of guys. I elbowed Heather to get her to look out the window and nodded toward him, "That one. I want that one."

We spent that day and night drinking and talking and flirting, and by the time we took a late-night walk to the beach, I was already done for. Sitting in the sand, giggling, I asked him, "What do I do with you?"

We fell right into being a couple — my first real relationship since high school and so, in some respects, my first ever. He was younger by a couple of years but possessed by a sureness and focus far more mature. Tall and dark and athletic, a boys' boy through and through — being the third born in a family of four brothers, but also simply by nature — and more confident than anyone else I knew. We became friends with each other's friends, and then our friends became friends, and the time between us was so easy and exciting and filled with the kind of bursting possibility that envelops you and delivers you into a different existence.

When we met that May, he was already set to go to law school in a different state in the fall. I proceeded all summer knowing this, but when September came, I was undone.

When he left for school, the question of whether or not we'd stay together was open. Neither of us knew how it would feel to be apart or what the first year of law school would demand. After three weeks on campus, he returned to Boston for a weekend. I was sick with nerves, wondering how we would be, hoping he'd missed me enough to erase all doubt. I met him on the street in front of my house that Friday, and when he got out of his car and looked at me, I knew by his expression that he had. The next year, he transferred to a school in Boston, and we moved in together. A year later, we were married, and the year after that, I got pregnant with Alma. We hadn't been trying, but we weren't preventing, either.

My drinking had been something of a surprise to us both. While we drank together and had fun with our friends and such, a darker undercurrent was building within me. He went from kindly asking me to slow down in the earlier days when the bad nights became more frequent, to outright screaming at me to fucking stop when it became clear how damaging it was to both me and our relationship.

When I drank a little, I wanted to make plans for our future; when I drank a lot, I picked fights and told him I wanted a divorce. At times, I was cruel and messy and volatile. At others, more like the girl he had met. Neither of us knew which one to believe. In the seven years we were together, we went through more than most people do in fifty. Financial hardship, multiple cross-country moves, family tragedies, death, mental illness, unemployment, job changes, becoming a family of our own. It's impossible to point to one thing as the primary cause of our downfall, but it's fair to say the drinking made everything worse.

Even so, at the end of it all, neither of us really knew how much trouble I was in.

As the phone rang, I thought about what I would say when Jake answered. I wasn't sure. I just desperately needed to hear a steady voice. By then, after almost two years separated, the rawness between us had been slightly eased by time. I couldn't tell him what had happened on Friday. He didn't know I was still struggling like this, and it would rightfully worry him too much, for Alma's sake. I counted two rings, then three, then four; then he answered.

As soon as I heard his voice, the back of my eyelids burned with tears. Big, salty pools of them.

I caught him up on the logistics of the weekend: little stories about Alma, new things she'd said or done. The stuff only he'd be interested in. He caught on that I was crying and asked if I was okay. I said I was, that I was just having a hard time, that it had been a long weekend. Despite all the mess between us, back then we were still each other's first call when something happened, even though we weren't sharing many of the details of our personal lives. He still knew me better than anyone else, and perhaps that was what I needed that morning: just to be known, for what I was before and underneath all this shit.

When we hung up, I sat up there a bit longer, looking across the city.

On the train, I held my backpack on my lap and closed my eyes. I was a girl dressed up as a grown-up.

More tears rolled down my cheeks, and I didn't even bother to try to stop them. The woman next to me handed me a Kleenex from her purse. God bless the people who carry Kleenexes in their purses. As I sat there crying, I remembered something from years ago, before Alma, before any of this. It was the end of a long day of my first yoga teacher training, and we were all gathered in a circle, asking questions, discussing the day. One of the students raised his hand and said, matter-of-factly, "I'm afraid I can't stop drinking."

The room went silent. All eyes went to our teacher, David.

Without missing a beat, he smiled, looked at him, and said, "Of course you can. Are you drinking right now?"

"No."

"And now?"

He smiled, and said softly, "No."

"...and how about right now?"

We all smiled this time.

"No."

This is how it is done — how anything is done. One moment, then the next, then the next. This is how this book is being written: I type this word, then this one, then this one. The words build sentences. The sentences build a paragraph. A book is impossible, but a word and then another word is not. A lifetime of sobriety was impossible, but a moment of sobriety was not. I was doing it, and I was doing it, and I was doing it again.

On that train ride, I did something new: I stopped promising myself I would never drink again. I didn't make any grand pronouncements; I didn't declare my intentions to anyone; I didn't send texts; I just sat there. I listened to Matt Berninger's baritone voice bellow in my ears as the train chugged toward the city.

I had been so tripped up by *forever*. By the idea of my entire life rolled out before me without a glass of silky red wine with my girlfriends, or a hoppy IPA on a deck, or a happy-hour cheers with my coworkers — *ever again*. Holidays, birthdays, summer, fall, winter, spring. What if I got married again? Finally traveled to wine country or back to Ireland or just down to New York? What if I dated someone who loved good whiskey or beer; what about the next big client dinner? Sure, I could make it through this week, or the next, and maybe even longer than that…but forever? What did that even mean?

After my first recovery meeting, a woman came over, took my hands in hers, and, with shining eyes, told me, "You never have to drink again!" I thought, *Is that supposed to make me feel better? Because it makes me want to die.* I didn't want to never drink again. I wanted to drink normally. Passably. Like I had before everything got fucked up. I'd assumed something was wrong with me because I didn't feel relief at her words. But nothing was wrong with me — I just wasn't there yet.

And I still wasn't there that morning on the train. So I stopped pretending I was. I stopped pretending, period.

I didn't commit to forever, or even tomorrow.

Just today. I wouldn't drink in this moment, or the next, or the next. I remembered something else a sober friend said to me: "If you want to drink tomorrow, you can. We can decide that tomorrow. Today, you don't, though. That's all."

It was the smallest resolve. The tiniest shift. Almost as if nothing had changed.

I don't remember how the rest of that day went, but I know I didn't drink. And now, nearly five years later, I still haven't. This isn't true because I said, *I will never drink again*. It's true — at least in part — because I said, *I will not drink right now, no matter what*, and I finally did everything necessary to be able to say that same thing in the next moment, and the next, and the next. Not because I was committed to forever, but because I finally realized the future was built on a bunch of nows, and that was it.

Every once in a while when I share this part of my story, someone will say to me, with a lot of animosity, "Oh, so you're saying we should just 'let what happens happen and not try to shape our life'?" My answer is no. That's not what I'm saying. What I'm saying is that anyone who knows the pain of purgatory knows there's no such thing as the future when the "right now" has you by the throat. I'm saying, for me, the arrogance of *I'll never drink again…* is the same arrogance that told me, *It's just one drink….* I'm saying you can drown in "forever" whereas you can wade into "right now."

In *The Power of Now*, Eckhart Tolle says, "Your outer journey may contain a million steps; your inner journey only has one: the step you are taking right now." I have found this to be true and helpful as it relates to doing a thing that at one time I was sure was impossible for me but that now I'm doing over and over and over again.

Day by day. Hour by hour. Moment by moment.

My thing is alcohol. But I am not drinking it.

I have friends who say they made the decision, and that was it. But that wasn't what worked for me. *Never, forever, always*: those words didn't make sense to me at all. They only caused my heart more despair.

Today, this moment, right now: those words I could do. Those words allowed me the space for everything else to exist, too. Like sadness. Frustration. Anger. Jealousy. Rage.

Not questioning the decision to be sober didn't work for me; I questioned it all the goddamn time. Because how was I to know that a life without drinking would actually be better? How did I know what it would mean for me? I didn't. Permission to question everything felt honest — and for a person like me, who had been pretending to be a lot of things she wasn't for as long as she could remember, that permission was necessary.

For a minute, imagine a life where you could tell the truth about what it is like to give up your thing. Imagine admitting how unfair it feels — that this comes so easily for everyone else and that it has wrecked you, over and over and over again. Imagine raging over all the pain it has caused you and raging, again, that you have to let go of the one thing that seems to get you through. Imagine being honest about all of that.

Then imagine, after all the thrashing, letting it go for a single minute.

Letting it be exactly as it is.

Imagine the relief.

I'll talk about how you have to set yourself up for success in your now decisions in the coming pages, I promise. But it's critical that I first give you permission to forget *forever*, because on that day, letting go of forever meant everything for me.

I think of David's words often: "Of course you can. Are you drinking right now?"

These words have carried me through more than just sobriety. They've carried me through massive life changes — transitioning into a new career, the first time I stepped onto a stage to share my story with a room full of strangers, making amends to people, getting through so many sleepless nights with my daughter. When I gave the eulogy at my grandma's funeral and my whole body went ice cold and trembled, I thought of David's words. When I had to break up with someone I cared for very much, I thought of David's words. When I started to peel back the layers of grief around my broken marriage and found myself in a fetal position on my bedroom floor, I thought of David's words.

No matter what you're asking yourself…

Can I give up my ex?

Can I stop abusing myself?

Can I stop using drugs?

…of course you can. Are you doing it right now?

Forget forever. It doesn't exist, anyway. As Eckhart Tolle also said, "It is not uncommon for people to spend their whole life waiting to start living," and that's exactly what you're doing when *now* is swallowed by projections of *forever*. Nothing in the future exists yet. But anything is possible right now. Including the thing you think you cannot do.

3

Stop Getting on the Train

The trouble with normal is that it always gets worse.

— BRUCE COCKBURN, "The Trouble with Normal"

It was hot for October. After the first two miles of my run, so much sweat was streaming off my body that my socks were soaked. I ran through the numbers in my head, calculating what I'd learned in marathon training: take the current outside temperature, add twenty degrees, and that's what it will feel like once you get moving. It was in the low seventies and humid as all hell, so I was running through ninety-degree soup.

Even worse, I was revving with panic.

It had been one month since my mom's birthday party, since talking to my brother outside the restaurant, and I still hadn't had a drink. I'd achieved that elusive thirty-day mark — thirty whole days of consecutive sobriety — for the first time since I started trying over a year prior. I walked down to the beach and used my fingers to sweep "30" in the sand, and I took a photo of it and posted it on Instagram. I thought maybe I would feel a sense of accomplishment, or a tiny bit of peace, but I felt just as raw and fragile as ever.

Every day was a long slog. So many people in AA seemed to be riding high in sobriety: confident, radiating joy, with energy to burn. Most days it was all I could do to get my body to and from my office in Boston, keep my kid alive, and not drink. I was all over the place: one minute, I'd feel electrified with hope and optimism, and the next, I'd be crying openly in public on the train to work. The fast-switching unpredictability of my mood and energy was so defeating, like being caught in one of those dreams where you're being chased and can't run; where you almost fly, but not high enough to keep the bad guys from grabbing you.

In hindsight, my life was insane then. It should have been exhausting, even *without* the monstrous task of overcoming an addiction.

I had a big job at a big marketing agency in downtown Boston, managing a team of six and several million dollars in business for my clients. I commuted an hour each way into the city every day and traveled nearly every other week for client meetings and pitches — sometimes only to New York but often as far as California or Hong Kong. Jake and I shared custody, so when I had Alma, I was managing a home and the dailiness of life with a five-year-old as a single parent: food shopping, clothes shopping, keeping toilet paper in the house, laundry, bathing, feeding, entertaining, paying the electric bill (and all the others), getting to bed, waking up, organizing, and delivering her to and from daycare and playdates and activities on the weekends.

Sometimes, our bathroom would start to resemble a porta-potty on the final day of a music festival or the trash bags would pile up by the door or my car oil light would blink at me angrily, and I'd realize I was actually waiting for Jake to take care of these things.

I was also a financial nightmare, so things were always getting shut off — my phone, the electricity, my credit cards. I was barely afloat, breathing through a straw.

I'd been using alcohol to hold things up on the back end for so long — and even though it had only made everything far worse, it offered the temporary illusion of escape and control. For a few hours every night, I didn't have to see or feel so sharply the mess.

Without the drinking, life should have become...easier. Everyone thinks it will be easier. But for me, and just about everyone I know, it was more like this:

Some days in those first thirty, I would be completely spent by the time I reached the office in the morning. Just getting myself and Alma ready and her fed and off to school — then doing the hour-long car/train/walk commute to work — was a whole day already. At night, I would text or call my sponsor, because that's what I'd been told to do. I'd often complain that I failed at doing anything productive that day.

"I literally just breathed and didn't drink. I sucked at everything else."

She would laugh, knowingly. "Well, babe, then you're a howling success."

That October day, I'd come home a little early from work, giving myself time to squeeze in a run before taking the train back into Boston. *If* I was going back. That decision had been swirling in my head since the Facebook invitation popped up in my in-box two weeks ago. It was my former boss's goodbye party — he was moving to California — and a group of my old coworkers were gathering at a bar downtown.

I wanted to go — or at least a large part of me wanted to go. Alma was with her dad for the weekend, for one, which always left me feeling like I should take advantage of the freedom. Looming larger in my mind, though, was my still-present resentment over the fact that "going out and drinking" had been the best avenue for new opportunities: meeting people, especially male people. Bonding. Having fun. I'd always loved the moment of that first glass-clinking "cheers" — a group's collective launch into celebrating, commiserating, diving into danger and mystery, pulling the rip cord on a workweek.

As bone-tired as I was, every invitation to something social sparked all those romantic ideas. So when the invitation showed up on Facebook and I saw the replies trickling in — "Yes!" "Can't wait!" "Oh boy!" — along with some inside jokes from our office and good-natured teasing of my boss, my brain flooded with the dopamine of that projected experience. And then, the mental gymnastics began.

I don't drink anymore.
I can't drink anymore.
What if...?
I can still go; it'll be fun!
No, it'll be awful.
I'll decide tomorrow.
Who in the group knows I'm not drinking? Will they be there?
What if I drink and then just start sobriety over again after?
What is the worst that will happen if I drink?
I won't go.

I will go and not drink.

I'll decide tomorrow.

I will go and drink a little, then leave.

Fuck it; I'm just going.

No! I can't go.

I'll decide tomorrow.

I'll ask someone sober to go with me so I have a sober buddy, like people keep suggesting.

Fuck that; that would be awful.

What will they think?

What will I miss?

What will I do if I don't go?

Will I end up sleeping with [x, y, z person] if I do?

I'll decide tomorrow.

OH MY GOD.

This debate had been running as the background track in my mind for two full weeks. I kept it to myself, despite admonitions from other sober people to discuss plans like this with a friend before making a decision. *Are you kidding?* I already knew what they'd say.

Consciously, I wasn't admitting to myself that I wanted to drink or planned on drinking. That would be preposterous considering...well...everything. But, back then, I still couldn't imagine myself going into that situation and enjoying it for even one moment without drinking. History proved that I wouldn't. And yet, saying no and counting myself out felt so impossibly unfair. I wanted to be able to do this kind of stuff. To have a life. To feel like part of the world.

As I dragged my sweaty, overheated body along the path, the voices intensified. As my body heat rose, so did the conflict — slowly at first and then faster and faster until the words had reached such a boiling point that I had to stop midstride. I lurched to a stop. All the energy drained from my body — an uncomfortably familiar sensation. And there I was standing dead-still on the sidewalk, gasping for air.

I'd been here before, the last time I had trained for the Boston marathon, in 2008.

I was married at the time, and I signed up on a whim — typical for me. I'd run it before, six years prior, and one day I got a surge of excitement about doing it again, so I committed. In the back of my mind, I also remembered how the long training runs on Saturdays kept me from drinking on Friday nights. Since high school, running had become a way for me to offset the internal chaos.

That time, the chaos stemmed from my sudden, confusing ambivalence about my marriage, how much I was drinking, and other things I could not name but only feel. I literally ran things off — burned them behind me, proving I was strong and capable. On weekend distance-training runs — twelve, sixteen, eighteen miles — I would leave Jake at home and set out for hours of meditative alone time. As I ran, my thoughts would inevitably pull me under, like an elevator dropping. Then, just like now, I would stop dead in my tracks and be gasping for air in the middle of the sidewalk.

Back then the thoughts went something like this:

I don't love my husband.

I am trapped.

I love my husband.

I am trapped.

I hate myself.

How could I?

Imagine if someone had filled your body with cement,

heavy and dense. As in they had emptied you out of everything that was soft and human and replaced all your organs and tissue with something…other. Something thick and rigid. Sometimes I would be running with a training group and someone in the group would see me — bent over, hands on my knees — and yell something well-meaning, like "You've got this!"

I'd try to force myself to cry so I could move again. Once, I screamed an animalistic "Fuck YOU!" at the ground, and a blast of white air exploded around my face because it was so cold outside.

Who was I yelling "Fuck YOU!" to? Who knows. Myself, mostly.

Eventually, I always moved forward again: one foot, then another, then another, turning up the music, willing myself to go on.

I was always proud of myself for the willingness to pick myself up off the side of the street and get the training run done. It tracked with my resolve to be "strong" like I had learned to do as a kid. Now, looking back, I wonder if this act of "discipline" was mostly just an act of self-aggression. I wonder if what I needed, more than to pick myself up and keep running, was to admit that I needed to stop. I wonder if what I needed was to ask for help. I wonder if this is what so many of us need when we think we need to get our shit together — to let it fall apart instead.

Today, as I ran that familiar path around the bay, I didn't stop to yell at the ground. I did stop to yell at the sky. And instead of yelling "fuck you," I looked up and screamed, "Stop! Stop! Just fucking stop!"

I couldn't take it anymore. The inner debate rang at fever pitch. I pinched my eyes closed. I could feel my heartbeat in my ears.

Fuck it, I thought. *I'm going.*

You know the feeling of seeing yourself do something you know you shouldn't do? Like you're watching yourself. You know the outcome will not be good. But you have lost the will to care. The adrenaline surges in, and your body acts out the next steps all by itself.

I finished my run, showered, picked out an outfit, and prepared for an evening out — makeup, blow-dried hair, and all. Meanwhile, my mind sped faster and faster. I checked the contents of my purse before leaving, and that was the first time I noticed my hands shaking. Hard.

I got in my car, and on the way to the train station, I pulled over at the liquor store. I bought a bottle of red wine, the screw-off kind, so I could open it on the train. The cashier put it in a brown paper bag, and I stuffed it into my purse. When I got to the station, my train was pulling up.

I needed something to hold the wine, so I grabbed the used Starbucks cup from my console and dumped the old coffee on the asphalt.

I hustled to the train.

I took a seat alone and pressed my sweaty forehead against the window. I brought my knees up against the back of the seat in front of me and rested them there so my feet were dangling like pendulums to the rhythm of the tracks. I closed my eyes for a beat while flashes of sun flickered through the autumn leaves and across my eyelids, creating a storm of red and gold. I breathed. I twisted the cap off the bottle.

When it comes to changing your life, there are these little moments of defiance like this. The moments that used to pass by gracefully without any fanfare but now scratch at you because you know too much. If I was going to drink now, it was going to be on purpose. There was a time when I would have opened that bottle with no hesitation and no regrets. None of the *Are you sure?* nonsense. But not anymore. Now, here I was riding this train even though I knew I didn't want to go where it was taking me, and I knew too much to stay on it. I didn't know how to get off.

Purgatory.

I thought of Holly. I thought of all the people in AA who had encouraged me to text them if I felt the urge to drink. I'd never followed this advice before; I always made my choice to start drinking again in the solitude of my own mind. I wasn't going to text any of them, but for some reason, I was willing to text Holly. One text. If she didn't answer right away, I would pour the wine into the cup.

Hi. I'm on the train and I'm flipping out. What's the meditation you said would help?

I waited. The little bubble appeared. *Shit.* She was writing back.

Hold on. Don't move, she said.

Then...

This is it.

She sent a link.

Do it and then text me back.

I hated meditating. I shake, twitch, scratch, get distracted by every noise, thought, task. I know this is supposed to be normal, but it feels torturous and the opposite of helpful.

I put in my headphones and turned it on. The voice, a woman's, directed me to breathe for a specific count, then hold my breath at the top, then breathe out, and repeat. I listened. I sat on my hands. My eyelids twitched, but I kept going. It was twelve minutes long. I didn't open my eyes. Not once. I did what I was told to do, and I hated it — every single moment.

Throughout the whole meditation, I held the bottle of wine between my legs.

When the meditation ended, I texted her back.

I'm doing it again.

I put the lid back on the bottle, stuffed it in my purse, and started the meditation again. I vaguely heard the conductor announcing stops. I felt the train slow and jerk forward. I kept riding, kept listening, kept breathing as instructed.

Suddenly, I sensed everyone around me getting up. We had arrived in Boston. I yanked my headphones out of my ears, grabbed my purse, and joined the stream of people leaving the train. As soon as my feet touched the station pavement, I knew what I had to do. I broke into a run. I flew through the station, weaving around the crowds of people and benches. When I reached the other side of the station, I stopped dead in my tracks the way I had done earlier during my run around the bay. I stared at the ground, then looked above me, as if to say, *What?* I pulled the bottle of wine out of my purse, along with the Starbucks cup.

I lifted both of them up above my head and slammed them into the garbage can beside me. The wine bottle made a loud, thick thud when it crashed into the bin, and a few onlookers turned. Then, silence.

It was over. I was panting.

I looked at the departures board for the next train back home: four minutes.

"Ma'am, do you want something?" I barely heard it at first, but when I looked up, I realized someone was speaking to me.

It was a guy behind the Sbarro pizza stand. "Oh, um. Sure, yes. Give me a slice of pepperoni. And a slice of cheese." I gave him money and walked with my greasy, hot slice-size boxes of pizza back to the train.

It wasn't until I stepped onto the train that I noticed all the unread messages on my phone. It was Holly.

Are you okay?

What are you doing?

Did it help?

Hello????

I texted her back.

Yes. Fuck. Thank you. I'm going home.

My whole body sank into the seat on my ride home. As I stared out the window, awash in postadrenaline fatigue, I felt as though I had no bones, no constitution left. I didn't eat the pizza. I didn't do anything. I'd walked right to the edge of the cliff and somehow, miraculously, hadn't fallen off.

I pulled safely into my parking spot at home, unscathed, less than two hours from when I left. The night I might have had — all that I had escaped — played out like a *Sliding Doors* scene. In two minutes, I could be in bed. Sober. There would be no inappropriate encounters, nothing to scrape from my memory or regret. No blurry fifty-dollar Uber rides home, or waking up elsewhere. No coming to at 3 AM with the uprush of terror in my throat. No new disasters. I felt like I had escaped a crash by a hair's breadth — I had.

How could I have come so close, again?

Why had the pull to get on that train been so otherworldly strong?

The answer to those questions, for me, felt like the difference between life and death.

"Babe, your brain was hijacked."

That was Holly's voice on the other end of the line. It was a day later now, twenty-four hours after the near disaster, and she had called to check in. When my phone rang, I was lying on my living-room floor with my legs propped up against the wall, staring at the ceiling — a yoga trick to try to smooth out my nerves. I put her on speakerphone and set the phone next to my head.

"Do you know that?" she asked, when I didn't answer.

"Yeah, I know," I said. I meant, I understood that I had lost it.

"No, listen," she said. "It really was. Do you get what's happening in your brain in those moments?"

"Ugh," I said. "Not really, I guess."

She explained: When we ingest a drug or a drink, our system instantly floods with an absurd amount of dopamine — from two to ten times the natural amount — causing an intense uprush of pleasure and focus, essentially shortcutting the brain's natural reward system. That feels really, really good.

Then a couple of things happen. The hippocampus — the part of the brain responsible for creating memories — lays down "tracks" or "records" of this rapid sense of satisfaction. So essentially the brain remembers: *I can cut straight to the good feelings with this simple little thing.*

Next, the amygdala, which is responsible for emotions and survival instincts, creates a conditioned response to the stimulus (for me, it's alcohol; for you, it's whatever your "thing" is), and as a result, the brain produces less dopamine or even in severe cases eliminates dopamine receptors in an effort to maintain balance, causing the activity that once used to be the fast track to pleasure to become less and less pleasurable over time.

Now, repeat this cycle a few thousand times, and the brain's reward and learning functions change significantly. The actual pleasure associated with the behavior subsides, yet the memory of the desired effect and the need to re-create it (the wanting) persists. The normal machinery of motivation no longer functions rationally.

"You were literally out of your mind," she said.

When we hung up, I did some rough math. If I drank alcohol two hundred days a year for fifteen years — that's three thousand revolutions of this powerful process. Three thousand "lessons" my brain cataloged. A blazing train down a neurological pathway of shame and regret. The drinking rewired my brain and primed it for more drinking. No wonder I felt crazy.

Take a minute and think about how many times you've walked the path of your "thing," whatever it is. No wonder you get on the train.

No wonder I got on the train.

I read somewhere recently that the word *addiction* is derived from a Latin term for "enslaved by" or "bound to," which makes perfect sense given how it functions. Because my brain had acquired such deep grooves of learning that an invitation to drink, like the Facebook invite to the party, for example, triggered the whole cycle into action. All the "positive" memories of drinking flooded back, my brain was set in motion, and there it was: an intense craving even though the pleasure of drinking had long gone.

All this is to say, notwithstanding my weeks of consecutive sobriety and hundreds of days in the year prior, regardless of my miles-long list of evidence proving drinking would yield horrible consequences for me, and despite such sure resolve in the days before, when I started imagining going to the party, my brain jumped on board the addiction train and started chugging away.

I try not to be harsh with that woman in me who jumped on the train. It's a fucking medical marvel she was able to jump *off* and make it home.

No one starts out drinking or using drugs (or gambling or having sex or shopping) with the intention of getting addicted. Most of us start wanting what everyone wants: to have some fun, feel more comfortable, feel *normal*. But after an indeterminable amount of exposure — and this part should terrify us since for some, just once is enough, and for others, it takes much more exposure — the process substantially changes our brain structure in primal, profound ways and we have boarded a train that will not let us off.

That day, as I lay on my floor and talked to Holly, a little piece of the puzzle snapped into place. While I'd heard so many times that I had become sick, that this wasn't my fault, that I didn't choose to become addicted, deep down I still suspected I was just weak and morally bankrupt. All the "it's not your fault" talk sounded like victim-mentality rationalization.

I had climbed through a lot in life, but not being able to control my downslide into addiction (and to consider myself addicted at all) — and then not to be able to just stop, given how grotesque the consequences had become — left me feeling like maybe I just didn't want to enough, like maybe I was actually just rotten and debased somewhere inside. And if that was true — if I was really just impossibly flawed, and no matter how hard I tried to stop drinking, I would never be able to do it — well...then what was the point of trying?

I remembered then something I'd heard in one of the first

meetings I went to in my hometown, more than a year before. An older woman shared a story about leaving her young kids home alone while she went to the bar to meet a man and not returning until the next day. They had no way to feed themselves, no one to put them to bed or keep them from wandering outside. It was a story you'd expect someone to sob telling, but she didn't — her expression remained soft and sincere, her tone even. She said it happened multiple times, and every time, she would beat herself to a pulp, wondering how on earth she could do that to her babies when she loved them so much.

She said, "What I didn't know is that addiction is stronger than love. Until it isn't."

This was what she meant. The addiction compulsion was otherworldly. And there's a reason it felt unnatural to deny it. It's because my brain was functioning as it *should*. Addiction was a learned behavior born of the natural, human impulse to soothe, to connect, to love, to feel good.

And if this was true, then I had to let my brain learn a new way.

I had to stop getting on the damn train.

The metaphor is so obvious, it almost hurts. That train was never going to take me anywhere but hell. That night, it was an actual train, but I had been metaphorically getting on the train ever since I'd first tried sobriety. And the whole time, I was thinking that the problem was with how I failed to manage the ride, not the decision to get on board in the first place.

I'd been getting on the train in so many ways:

- Going to happy hours
- Going to restaurants where I used to drink
- Replying "yes" or "maybe" to any get-together or party

that reminded me of my drinking life instead of just declining right away

- Going to concerts
- Listening to certain music (you know, like the music you and your ex loved together)
- Getting on dating apps and not indicating I was sober
- Getting on dating apps
- Going on dates with men who didn't know I was sober
- Going on dates
- Taking the train home from work, which required me to pass through the train-station bar where I'd sat drinking hundreds of times
- Driving my old route home from work, which took me past the liquor store where I used to stop in and get wine for the second half of the drive
- Texting with men I used to drink with
- Texting most men
- Traveling for work and attending the happy hours and dinners
- Traveling for work (or for anything) without a serious plan of accountability to sober people
- Traveling without the people I was traveling with knowing I was sober
- Doing anything without the people I was with knowing I was sober
- Following friends on social media who regularly posted about drinking
- Not making specific, sober plans on Friday and Saturday nights
- Not checking in with sober people every day
- Taking my daughter to dinner at restaurants where they served alcohol

- Walking through the areas of Boston where I lived in my twenties

You might be reading this and thinking, *WTF, did you have to shut down your entire life? Do I have to shut down my entire life?*

And the truth is: Yes. Yes, I did. I had to shut down everything within my power that my brain had connected to drinking. For a while. I had to do it until new tracks were made. (Okay, I know you want a timeline — we all want a timeline. It's different for everyone, but it's safe to say that it's going to take longer than you want. For me, it took a couple of years.)

Whether or not you need to do the same is for you to decide, but I'll tell you this: Each time I said no to "getting on the train" — whatever that looked like in the moment — I created a new space. Sometimes that space was a fraction of a millimeter, barely perceptible. Sometimes it was huge, the size of oceans. In the spaces I found loneliness. Emptiness. Fear. Confusion. Grief. I often believed there was no end to the space. I worried I was being punished, and I often also believed I deserved to be.

But eventually, after the night or the weekend or the hour of acute discomfort had passed, I realized that…well, it had simply…*passed.*

It had passed.

And in the wake of the passing, in the new space, I found a burst of strength. A bit of integrity. A modicum of belief that I could change. Maybe I wouldn't have to be afraid of myself all the time anymore. I could make good choices. I was building something, and it was new and pink and required the seriousness and protection of a newborn life. Whatever it took to keep the baby alive, so to speak — that's what I did.

It is practical and profound at the same time: you stop getting on the train long before it pulls into the station. You make the choices you have the capacity to make in the moment so that you don't have to try to fight the ones beyond your power down the line. You decide to stay in the empty space — desolate as it may be — for as long as it takes to turn that tiny pink thing into something viable and stronger, with power and weight.

And it will. Your life will inevitably turn into something more viable and bigger and richer than the promise of anything on that train. That ride, as a matter of fact, will cease to be interesting at all.

4

Find a House
Where the Truth Is Told

I thought I was alone who suffered.
I went on top of the house,
And found every house on fire.

— BABA SHEIKH FARID

The very first AA meeting I attended was at noon, a short walk from my office in Boston's financial district, in a dusty room on the third floor of a building facing Boston Common. I'd looked it up on the Massachusetts AA website, so I knew it was a women's step meeting, though I had no idea what that meant. Kacey, a dear old friend from college who'd resurfaced when I was pregnant with Alma, said it should be a good first meeting to try. "Don't make up your mind until you go to at least a dozen different meetings, though, okay?"

It was so hot and humid that day that my violet dress was stuck to my thighs after the five-minute walk. Only one woman was there when I arrived. It was a small but natural light–filled room lined with built-in bookshelves on the walls, and windows facing the park. It smelled like the church downstairs and also library books. No AC. She was setting up a small round table by arranging folding chairs around it and placing a book down for each person. I strode toward the table like I knew what I was doing and grabbed a seat.

Slowly, a few more women trickled in. They all seemed to know each other: they exchanged hellos or nodded at each other; some hugged. When the clock hit noon, we began. I followed along as best I could while someone who introduced herself as the meeting chair read an opening preamble, made announcements, read from a few different laminated sheets, then asked everyone to introduce themselves. In total no more than eight women were there, most of them much older than I was, including one who had been sober for an impossible thirty-five years — almost as long as I'd been alive.

I tried to stay open but couldn't stop thinking that this could not possibly be my life.

I've tried to write this chapter at least four times now. I've thrown away over ten thousand words trying to get it right. Trying to cover a topic that feels too big to cover in a single chapter — or maybe even a single book. Because it's not about AA, not really. It's about the whole of my recovery. AA is to my sobriety as my marriage was to my heart — it is an avenue through which I explored a becoming, but not my ultimate destination. A place I pushed against, fell into, examined, embraced, accepted, rejected, and projected all my limitations and smallness onto and the big, beautiful stuff, too.

It was my first harbor after the biggest shipwreck of my life, which means it will always be invaluable, because without it, I'm not sure there would have been anything beyond the shipwreck. AA gave me space to grow, even when I wasn't all in, because it gave me a baseline — a home I could be sure of — even when I wandered. As Freud wrote in a letter to his fiancée, "How bold one gets when one is sure of being loved." Yes, perhaps that was what AA gave me most of all: a place to be bold, a place to push against.

As I write, I keep questioning my motivation. Many people told me not to broach the subject of AA because it can be polarizing, but that's exactly why I *am* broaching it.

As in politics and religion, the beliefs on both extremes of AA are dangerous and limiting. There are those who live and die by the program and can't objectively hear any criticism without jumping into a dogmatic slogan-slinging fit. And there are people on the other extreme, who believe the program is a cult and only a cult. Neither of those perspectives is helpful or true; reality is always much more nuanced.

I once heard a clinical psychologist talk about his philosophy on antidepressants. He said, "If someone comes to me and they're clinically depressed, it's almost always a good idea to get them on antidepressants. *Why?* Because if they die, I can't help them." At the most basic level, simply because of its current prevalence and reach, AA can be the first point of contact for someone who is in deep shit like I was. And for all its failings and imperfections — and there are many, and they are real — the people in AA saved my life. They helped me get my first thirty days of sobriety; then later, in my third year of sobriety, doing the steps saved me again. And — all the while — *I didn't buy into it all.* I still don't. It's okay for things to be complicated. That's what I want you to hear, maybe more than anything.

Kacey was the only friend I'd talked to about my drinking through the years. We'd been college roommates at Colorado State; she'd arrived my freshman year, two years older than everyone else, having toured in Europe as a model before starting school. We both got fake IDs and quickly realized we drank the same way.

Almost everyone drinks hard in college, but budding problem drinkers have a spidey-sense for each other: we drink with an intent that's only perceptible to someone on the same frequency.

After college, we communicated here and there over email and text but mostly fell out of touch. Around 2008, we reconnected on Facebook and soon started chatting over Messenger. My catch-up: I was newly married, living in South Boston, and pregnant. Hers: she was living in Georgia, she and her boyfriend had a two-year-old daughter, and she'd been sober for almost a year.

I had a million questions, naturally. She answered them without hesitation or pretense. There had been a messy fight between her and her boyfriend that turned into an arrest, a brief stay in jail, and then rehab. Not being able to see her daughter while she was in jail and rehab did her in. She surrendered, she told me. Went to AA, got a sponsor, went through the steps, and hadn't looked back. She was grateful.

Neither of us was surprised things had gone that way.

My curiosity piqued over Kacey's story, as it did over all addiction stories. My bookshelf was proof: memoirs were stacked there like a small, private support group — Anne Lamott, Mary Karr, Caroline Knapp, Stephen King, Pete Hamill. If asked, I would have said I loved any redemption story, and that would have been true — but in those voices and stories I recognized something specific about myself. I wanted to know every little detail of their inner lives, their missteps, how much they drank, and when and why and what it cost them.

The common thread in all these stories, and in Kacey's, and in that of my dad — who stopped drinking for ten years when I was fifteen — and in every anecdotal tale of problematic drinking (labeled *alcoholism* across the board, always) that I knew of was Alcoholics Anonymous. The twelve steps. If this was your thing, that's where you went. It was a foregone conclusion.

This was the repeated trajectory, as I understood it and as it's most often represented in culture: bottom, surrender, AA, sponsor, steps, recovery, gratitude. It sounded sweet, but…I don't know. Trite. Too simple.

From the beginning of our reconnection, Kacey dropped hints. "Your turn," she'd say with a wink in a text. I'd only hinted to her about the state of my drinking — usually after a really bad night when my defenses were down and I was scared. But she didn't need me to fill in the details for her. She'd lived all the stories, too.

When I slept my way through my train stop the morning after a horrible night and returned home at one thirty in the afternoon to a very angry and worried husband, Kacey heard about it. When I blacked out at my company's holiday party and had to be ushered to my hotel room by my boss and later spoken to by the CEO, Kacey heard about it. When I drove drunk with Alma in the car and woke up terrified, Kacey heard about it. When I ended up doing drugs with strangers and waking up in places I didn't recognize, with no recollection of having gone there, Kacey heard about it. And after Alma's birth when I was so racked with crippling anxiety that I could no longer eat but yet found myself drinking wine every night even though it just made me worse, Kacey heard about it.

Every time, Kacey would gently but firmly offer what she'd learned: that it would never get better on its own; that this was a spiritual sickness, not just a mental and physical one; that I didn't have to live this way; and that a sober life would be better than anything I could imagine. After each new low, she would ask me if it was enough. Sometimes I said it was, but only because I knew it was the right answer, not because it was the truth.

"Just go to a meeting, girl. Try it."

I listened, but I never thought I would actually set foot in a meeting. I don't know how else to explain that other than to say I just couldn't imagine a reality where I'd actually have to set the intention to stop drinking alcohol. Even when my nights started to match the ones I read about in the books. Even when I got the DUI. Even when I struggled to put mascara on in the morning because my hands shook so terribly. Even when I started to notice a tinge of yellow behind the angry red capillaries in my eyes, an indication of liver damage.

Kacey would share her own experiences. She would listen to my thoughts and answer the questions I'd already asked a dozen times: "What exactly did it feel like to you? How do you feel now? Is sobriety actually better? Why?"

Finally, the morning after my brother's wedding, Kacey said: "I think this is enough of a bottom, girl. Don't you?"

And I did. Of *course* I did.

But I still couldn't wrap my head around walking into a meeting.

I told myself I'd find one when I got home from the wedding and settled a little. But in the first few days back, I started to detox — something I hadn't anticipated. I'd had no idea I was drinking enough to experience such a potent withdrawal, or that the worst symptoms came not hours after the last drink but days later. In a moment of terror that perhaps I'd actually caught some kind of deadly flu (since these sensations couldn't possibly be caused by four days without alcohol), I googled "alcohol withdrawal" from my bathroom floor in the middle of the night.

Racing heart, fever, heavy sweating, hallucinations, disorientation, vomiting, severe shaking, seizures. Minus the seizures, everything else was right. I did not have the flu. I was going through a process that I later learned can be fatal.

It took every ounce of my remaining life force just to survive those few days, and I'm still not sure how I did it without a psychotic collapse. I wasn't sleeping at all, but I dragged myself to work and barely managed to function.

Adding an AA meeting was too much to manage, I told myself.

Then a couple of weeks passed, and the horror of what had happened in Colorado started to fade. Though I didn't start drinking again yet, I could feel myself stealthily entertaining the possibility. As the days clicked on, I could feel my thoughts around drinking slide from a very black-and-white "no fucking way" to a little grayer "well…maybe…" and that shook me.

So, I ran out of my office during lunch that day in Boston, dress sticking to thighs, to join women gathered around a tiny table, sharing stories.

I wanted so badly to hear something of myself in each of

those women's shares, but I just couldn't. I felt too young, too smart, too pretty, too complicated.

The part of me that knew I was supposed to be humble kept reminding me to be grateful, not to judge, not to assume, not to hate that this might be my new reality. But inside I was dying. *No fucking way*, I thought, even as I smiled and nodded and said, "Thank you."

"Thank you" when they offered me tissues after I shared.

"Thank you" as they pressed their phone numbers into my palm after the meeting.

I felt a tiny slice of relief having gone, though. While a future that included regular attendance seemed as alien as anything, at least it wasn't all a complete unknown anymore. It had been really hard to get myself there, but I'd done it. I sat there and said impossible words. I could tell Kacey I went. I knew where to go next week. It was something.

I wish I could say I never touched alcohol again after that meeting, but that's not how the story goes, as you've probably figured out by now. Over the next couple of months, I continued to show up there, and I tried out a few other meetings, too. Sometimes going helped tremendously, like taking the edge off a blinding migraine, but other times I felt only more desperate and angry when I walked out.

At first, I went by myself — usually showing up late and running out the door immediately after the meeting ended. More than once, I went straight home afterward and drained two bottles of wine in some kind of out-of-body trance. But usually I picked up a little something helpful. I saw the faces of other people who were doing the same thing. I accumulated tiny bits of new experiences that — whether I welcomed them or not — started to stick.

For months, I kept everything compartmentalized. Sobriety was a background activity I was working at while I tried to carry on with the rest of my life as if nothing had changed. Except for the people who were invested in my sobriety — Jake, my mom, my brother, a couple of friends — I didn't talk to anyone else about it. I didn't engage with people at meetings. I picked apart people's words when they shared. Occasionally, I promised myself I would stay afterward and try to talk to someone, but every time, I got spooked and scrammed out the door.

Eventually, after drinking my way through a work trip to London and subsequently getting reprimanded by my boss, I decided I'd better dig in a little more. So I went to a new meeting — the biggest one in Boston — and promised myself I wouldn't leave without talking to a woman, any woman, and asking her to be my sponsor.

That night, just like every other time I got over myself and stopped being so picky about how I got help, something changed. At that meeting, I met Allison, who agreed to be my temporary sponsor and eventually became my real sponsor. She introduced me to a whole crew of people and showed me the best meetings.

It was a start.

⬤

The most important thing that happened in that first year of going to meetings was this: I heard people tell the truth. Before I walked into that first meeting, nobody — not even my ex-husband, who had lived with me for eight years — knew how much I was drinking. And really, since I'd started drinking twenty years before, I'd been privately storing away the shame I felt about it, how much I relied on it, how much thoughts of drinking or not drinking had consumed me. Even I hadn't acknowledged those things.

I had created a totally separate internal world that didn't match my outsides, and this incongruence left me feeling terribly alone, even when I was surrounded by people.

I had been carrying around one million heavy secrets and was convinced I always would. As it turned out, those secrets were not just mine.

In the meetings, I saw myself in dozens of different faces: all the houses on fire, to quote the epigraph from the start of the chapter. Nothing is such balm for a broken soul as this — to know you are not alone.

And so, even if I agreed with nothing else, I found others who occupied the same quadrant of hell as I did. I heard people describe my inner life when they shared theirs. And even when I rejected their methods, their honesty alone breathed fresh air into the dark, twisty parts of me that had been so long knotted up.

Over the course of about a year, despite myself, I grew to know a pretty large circle of sober people, mostly in AA and a few who weren't — like Holly. Some became close friends, some were acquaintances, and many were just familiar faces. But by all, I was known as a person who was trying to get sober. A new identity was forming, and its foundation — unlike all the others I'd built and destroyed over time — was rooted in the most naked, honest space of my being.

Even though I hardly ever wanted to go, I started getting invited to sober things. Parties. Dinners. Coffee. 10Ks. Ski trips. People kept saying, "Come hang with us," and even if I didn't go or even want to, it was really nice to be asked.

When I got up the nerve to admit I was angry about every-thing, uncomfortable as fuck, and sad, they nodded. I didn't have to explain. They told me to call whenever and picked up their phones when I did and didn't ask why I was calling. They smiled when I showed up at a meeting after going missing for a few weeks and didn't say "Where have you been?" but instead "It's so good to see you."

Anne Lamott talks about how at some point in her recovery process, she'd developed relationships with so many people who were invested in her sobriety that she couldn't just disappear anymore. If she went off the radar for more than a day or so, she'd get calls, or people would show up at her house. She called them "The Interrupters." I eventually created a crew of inter-rupters myself. They kept tabs on Laura. They sent texts and called. They kept inviting me to things. They didn't let me dis-appear, even when I tried. They kept me accountable, which I eventually learned was a wise and necessary thing, not the insult to my sovereignty I'd once perceived it to be.

I was held. This was not about a doctrine or methodology but about finding a space where I could be seen, if I wanted — and allowed to just be.

I think I've made this clear, but it was not all a lovefest. Many people in AA drove me fucking crazy. I often found myself press-ing the palms of my hands into my eye sockets during a meet-ing, *willing* someone to stop talking. I walked out of meetings because I just couldn't listen to the drivel someone was spewing for one more second. I wanted to punch people right in the face for being so dogmatic, depressing, or exhausting. Some men were creepy. Some women were petty (and creepy). Sometimes

it felt like the worst parts of high school, all cliquey and inse-
cure. I loathed the idea of being twenty years sober and *still*
going to meetings, hearing the same stories — telling the same
stories — and the repeated notion that if I didn't go to meetings,
I would fall into drinking again. I didn't buy that all my problems were because I was an alcoholic — I found that absurd. I
didn't even *call* myself an alcoholic outside of the meetings, and
not because I had any illusions about whether or not drinking
was a problem for me but because I found it — still find it —
punitive. And while the God thing wasn't a barrier for me, as it
is for many, I had a hard time reconciling the insistence that this
was a disease *and* that this was the one disease that only God
could cure. *Really?*

Many times, when I wanted to argue my way out of sobriety, I threw the baby out with the bathwater and told myself the
whole thing was idiotic and not for me. I told myself I didn't
need it, that I'd do it alone — my way. I decided that all these
people were idiots, and I bounced. Inevitably, I would end up
drinking again. And eventually, I'd end up back at a meeting or
texting/calling someone from AA because I didn't know what
else to do.

Again, for better or worse, I didn't have anywhere else to go.

In the year that followed my initial meeting, I was drinking
far less, except that when I did drink, it was darker, scarier, and
more secretive. I totaled my car. I blacked out and drove in the
middle of the night. I never knew what was going to happen
anymore once I started. I knew if Alma's dad found out I was
drinking like that, I risked losing custody of her. My job was in
danger, too.

Another thing happened over time, though. I saw people
whom I'd met when we were both new get their six-month,

nine-month, and one-year chips. I saw people get better, or at least stop drinking, which both showed me it was possible and also slapped me awake. After a year, I still hadn't pulled together thirty consecutive days. My excuses were so good and real and justified. And yet, I knew most of my resistance was an argument against being sober, not AA itself.

During this time, I often thought of a phrase my friend Brooke said to me when she was going through a divorce. Her husband had a years-long affair, and when they were separating, he kept picking at certain details of their history — like how they'd spent Christmas ten years before — that seemed irrelevant to her given the bigger picture. She said, "It's like he's arguing about the furniture when the house is burning down."

It occurred to me at some point that nitpicking about AA was also a little bit like arguing about the furniture while the house was burning down. I figured that after I had actually been sober for some time, like maybe a year or two, I could critique things then and decide to stay or go. Until then, the reality was this: meetings provided me with a safe place to be, the people there were the only sober community I had, they were willing to hold me through this process, and I had to admit that *maybe* people who'd actually walked this path might have something to teach me.

So, I started paying less attention to how I felt about AA and more attention to the facts: was I still drinking, or not? I took a few suggestions: soliciting a sponsor, texting or calling sober people every day, going to more meetings. And over time, it grew to be something like a long-term relationship when you've reached that place where your commitment to the thing — the respect and reverence for the larger whole — trumps the inevitable and lesser ups and downs. The benefits started to drastically outweigh the costs.

Specifically, I found a couple of meetings that I liked, and I stuck to them. One was a noontime meeting in Boston that was mostly men. The other was a Saturday-night beginners' meeting in my hometown. I let people get to know me, and I started to know them. I got used to seeing their faces and looked forward to hearing about their lives. I joined, in my own way. And I realized my identification with the community didn't have to come at the price of my individuality.

It's probably the most overused aphorism in AA, but I abide by it — and not only in relation to AA but as it applies to all of life: "Take what works, and leave the rest."

There was so much wisdom and beauty to be gained in those gatherings, and when I focused only on who and what was useful, the rest didn't rub me so badly, or at least I didn't have to take that rub so personally and seriously. I could reject whatever the hell I wanted so long as I was staying sober.

In July 2014, a full year after I'd started going to AA, I went to a sober party in Boston — with Alma and a bottle of vodka in the car. I'd been drinking much of that day, and I can't explain my decision to go to that party with my daughter any more than I can explain any other decisions I made while drinking.

Shocker, but it didn't take too long for people to figure me out. And when they did, all that happened was this: a few people kindly ushered me outside, gathered up my daughter, elected someone to drive, and took us home. A woman whom I'd met only once or twice drove us forty-five minutes north of the city to my home without saying one unkind or judgmental word, and then she drove forty-five minutes back.

She just got us home safe. No questions asked. The end.

It took me a while to even acknowledge what had happened when I saw the people from the party, and some I never had the nerve to talk to again. Writing these words, I can still feel it all over my body: the heat of the shame, the urge to cover my face, my heart sinking into my chest. I know I don't need to feel that way anymore, but believe me when I tell you it's *not* a common occurrence for people to show up drunk at an AA party. And I had my daughter with me. And I drove.

They got me home. They loved me. They loved her.

It's been five years, and it still makes me squirm to think about that night. It was one of those things I thought I'd just lock up in a box and never write about. But I'm telling you because for any kind of critique I could write about these people or this program, there will always be that night, and other times, too, in which I was held so tenderly and without question.

If there is anything it takes to heal, it's that. Find those people — wherever they are. Let yourself be held in undeserved favor.

And I can tell you that it happened that way not because those people are saints but because they learned service in those meetings and in that program. Most of them were probably just passing on what had been done for them, even if they didn't want to. That's what is taught. And because they did it, I lived and was safe, and so was my daughter. Because they did it, I did the same in the years that followed.

So, underneath any junk I may have about AA, there is that night, and all the other moments I was carried, impossibly, and there is the lesson that I will never lose and that will contribute to my life and my peace inextricably, forever: *put yourself in a house where the truth is told.* I don't care if it's in the rooms of AA or somewhere else. What I know is such a place exists for you — be it a room full of people or in the heart of just one other human to start. Find that place. Go out onto the roof. See all the other fires. And stay there. Stay, until you are carried to the shore of a different life — until you become a house of your own.

5

Push Off from Here

*There is a time for departure
even when there's no certain place to go.*

— Tennessee Williams, *Camino Real*

I shoot up in bed and scan my surroundings. I've done this a thousand times since I've been sober — a trained response from all the times I woke up in a place I did not recognize, with a crushing headache and anxiety coursing through me as though I was on fire from within, as I tried to piece together the night.

This morning, everything is fine. I am sober. In my bed. Everything is in its place.

I lie back down, and a memory flashes into my mind: a morning from those first shaky months of trying to stop, but failing. Alma is sleeping next to me this morning, like she was then, but everything else is different. This morning the house is quiet and warm. That morning the apartment was dark, and strangely freezing, even for a winter day. That morning I could smell the wine in my nose, oozing from my pores, everywhere. I can still smell it now — I think it will remain indelible on my brain for the rest of my life.

That morning my head was throbbing, and dizziness flooded over me. I winced and let the waves of pain roll through.

I went through the details of the situation in my head.

Okay, so you drank last night.

Okay.

Okay.

It's okay.

I willed myself not to panic, hoping I could stave off the anxiety attacks that often came the morning after. I touched Alma's body, making sure she was breathing — a morbid thing, but true. *No damage done*, I told myself, though I hadn't seen my phone yet. *Don't pick it up yet*, I told myself. *Just breathe.*

I kept coaching myself.

I will drink water, take some Advil, and go back to sleep. Sleep in a little, even. It is Saturday.

It is still incredible to me the amount of horror we can withstand in active addiction. The constitution or sheer dissociation it requires to move through such moments — knowing you have done it again, have broken your own heart again, have played Russian roulette with your very life. The physicality of it alone is horror — the aching body, the racing heart, and in my case, always throwing up my insides violently. It is the stuff of living hell. But the spirit: I just don't know how it goes on.

When I stood to get out of bed, I realized why the room was such a frigid temperature. The window to my room was wide open, and snow was blowing outside and scattering on the floor beside the sill.

I shoved the pane down to close the window and a gust of bitter wind whipped up through my T-shirt. I walked toward the kitchen, where I assumed I must have left my phone. But when I turned on the hallway light, I let out a gasp. The white walls, floorboards, and floor were stained with sprays of deep red and vomit. There were shards of broken glass, stained with red wine, everywhere. My jeans and black suede boots were tossed on the floor, caked with the contents of my stomach. The smell hit me, and I remembered.

I had bought wine on the way home from picking up dinner at Panera — two bottles of twist-off cheap red — while Alma waited in the car. I promised myself, as I always did, that I wouldn't drink them both. Then, of course, when both were gone, I decided I needed more. So with Alma asleep, I got dressed in the jeans and boots that were now on the floor in front of me and drove to get more. After that, the evening is only a blur, but I do recall getting sick. All over the walls, the hall, all over myself.

I started rushing to get everything back in order. I tiptoed around the glass to the kitchen to grab supplies: dustpan and brush, paper towels, 409 cleaner. I lifted my boots and jeans up from the floor. I tossed the boots outside — I'd just bought them, and they were ruined. My jeans went in the wash, and I started the water. Hot. Lots of detergent.

How are we still doing this, Laura? How? I wasn't the girl of two years ago anymore, before the DUI, before my brother's wedding, when the denial was still so thick that it's fair to say I wasn't even *lying* to myself about how bad it had become. I'd been going to meetings for over a year; I had all the knowledge; I had a sponsor; I even had an Instagram account talking about sobriety. And yet, here I was again.

I struggled to collect all the glass because it was wet with wine, and the brush kept getting wet and uncooperative, but I kept trying. My heart was still hammering against my chest like a manic prisoner. I switched tactics and scooped up the glass shards with globs of paper towels, catching the still-wet vomit and wine, too. Three or four rounds of this, and then I swept it all into the dustpan.

Now I moved on to the walls and floorboards. I started by spraying the 409 directly on the wall. The cleaner pulled away some of the stains but mostly bleached the walls a grayish purple. I kept scrubbing furiously when a voice came from behind me.

"Mama, what're you doing?"

There was Alma, standing in the hallway. There she was with her little sleep-fresh body, her blue eyes, her sweet powder-blue-and-white pajamas. Five years old.

"Hi, honey. I don't know. I don't know what happened," I lied.

"Did someone break into the house?"

"I don't think so, baby. I'm just trying to clean it up — you can go back to sleep."

"Oh no, Mama. I think someone must have come in!" She came closer and grabbed a paper towel. "I will help."

Does she know? Am I really going to let her believe that someone broke into the house?

I couldn't muster another explanation.

"Thanks, baby, that's so sweet of you. But you don't need to help," I told her, but I also didn't stop her. I needed her to believe this didn't happen the way it did as much as she needed to believe she wasn't in danger.

We both pretended.

I stared at her little hand holding the wet paper towel, rubbing in vain against a stain of red she didn't understand. It was too much.

It's still too much.

"I'll do it, sweetie. Stop," I said, and it wasn't until it was out of my mouth that I realized I sounded angry. Alma was, of course, confused. Seeing my mistake, I moved toward her and scooped her up. "I'm sorry, sweetie. I'll take care of it; let's go back to bed."

I waited until Alma was asleep again before I went out to finish the job. Because the floorboards had a glossy finish, the stains mostly came up. The walls, on the other hand, were permanently inked. The purplish gray of the bleached stains made the walls look kind of dirty from afar, but up close the shape of the stains gave it away. Dirt doesn't splatter; liquid does. The stains stayed there until I moved out a year and a half later.

As I sat on the floor cleaning the walls, I listened anxiously for any sound indicating Alma was waking up again. My mind played a video montage of all the times my drinking had hurt her. They are the deepest grooves of my shame, the unspeakable bits of my story.

I drank when I was pregnant with her — not enough to necessarily be considered too much, but it was the wanting to drink more that haunted me. And I always wondered, *Maybe it was too much?* I googled "fetal alcohol syndrome" so many nights, trying to search for proof that she would be okay.

I joked throughout the pregnancy that I couldn't wait to jump off the cliff of sobriety once she was born, and I did, went straight back to it.

I breastfed her after having too much, and I gave up after three months, partly because my body wasn't producing enough milk and every time she latched on, it felt like razor blades on my nipples, and partly because I didn't want to have to worry about polluting her anymore.

I drove with her countless times buzzed and drunk. One time, a couple of years before, we were leaving a beach party and I was urging her to climb into the back seat. I swung the car door open a little too fast, misjudging where she was in relation, and the edge of the door hit her in the corner of the eye. She cried hysterically. I told myself it was something that could happen anytime.

I slept next to her, or under the same roof, unconscious. If she had needed me in the middle of the night, I would likely not have heard her or been able to react quickly.

I read her bedtime stories while sipping wine, and often drunk.

I gave her baths while sipping wine, and often drunk.

I drank through birthdays, holidays, playdates, and parties, telling myself it was all innocent and what I *deserved*.

I chose going out and partying over being at home with her.

And then, of course, there was my brother's wedding. I am sure you want more details about this, or I suspect you do. I've written the scene dozens of times, each time more gutting than the last, and I've decided to leave it out. What's important is that it happened. And afterward, I finally saw the stark, simple equation:

I almost lost my daughter because I was drinking.

And not only "lost" as in she might have been taken from me, but she could have been picked up by someone as she was wandering the halls of the hotel alone, looking for me. She could have become sick. She could have hurt herself. She could have died. She was only four years old.

Until then, I could always blame the severity of my inebriation and the consequences of my drinking on other factors: not eating enough, other people, medication, an event, the stress of my life, a bad night. I could play things down, or — if it was only I who knew — simply brush them under the rug. But not this. There were no "complicating factors" even though there were many. It wasn't just a bad night. The truth was — and had been for a long time — I never knew what was going to happen once I started drinking. Anything was possible. And after that night I couldn't pretend otherwise.

As I was cleaning the wine off the walls, I remembered what a woman at that first AA meeting had said to me. Because it was a round-robin-style meeting and there were so few of us, I'd spoken. I told them about the wedding, about Alma, about how I never knew what was going to happen anymore when I started drinking, and that it had been that way for a long time, but I'd been too afraid to admit it.

At the end, when we were packing up, a woman my age, with a red, puffy face and too-tight ponytail she'd pulled back when her hair was still wet, approached me.

"I have a daughter, too," she said, "and I get it, what you're feeling."

I nodded. More tears.

"I know, I know," she continued, touching my arm lightly and looking straight at me. "It's the absolute worst. But you need to know, you can push off from here. You can leave all that behind."

I thanked her and left.

Those words stuck with me: *Push off from here.*

Those words provided a surprising amount of relief in that acute moment. What I took from it then was that I didn't have to stay mired in my self-hatred, that it would drown me if I did. Things could be different, starting now. Part of the reason I'd kept drinking, even if subconsciously, was because it seemed unimaginable to face all the wreckage.

Thawing out to the reality of your life, especially if you've hurt a lot of people, ruined relationships, and dug yourself into a gnarly financial or employment ditch — a reality for many people who are addicted and certainly the reality for me — can simply be too much to face at once. It's emotionally and logistically crushing. Where does one start? Is it even possible to rebuild? How? And how long does it take?

Even if you make solid progress early on, it is so easy to become overwhelmed again, to say another "fuck it all," to figure you can just begin again at some elusive, illusory date in the future, when you're stronger and have more resolve. Even if you are the kind of drinker whose damage has largely been internal — the insidious rattle of anxiety, the slow disintegration of your connection to people and things, the undertow of regret that you might not be living as you could — it can be tough to stay afloat when the tides of what you have repressed begin to roll in.

That morning, facing Alma, I thought of those words again: *you can push off from here.*

Meaning: This was horrible. Truly awful. But I could also push off. It could be my starting place. I never had to feel this way again.

At first, I understood it only as permission. I thought the

woman was saying, *You're allowed to move forward from here. You don't have to look at all that horrible shit right now.* I desperately needed to hear that, because in that moment, I was drowning.

What I've come to know is that it's possible, and actually necessary — especially in the beginning of sobriety — to take responsibility for your experience without looking at everything awful you've done right away. I thought I had to fall on the sword for everything I'd ever done. Immediately. Which kept me drinking, in some sense, because it was all just too much.

What she meant was that I didn't have to face all of it at once. Couldn't, in fact. That it was okay for me to be here. Figuring it out. Right where I was.

I don't know what comes to mind for you when you hear me tell a story like this, but I know you have your own unspeakable parts. If you're a parent, too, that's probably where they live. As my friend says, "There's a special kind of vitriol saved for mothers who become addicted." Whatever it is for you, I'm giving you the same permission right now: you can push off from here. You don't have to look at it all right now; you can't. It is probably too soon. You're probably not ready. There is definitely time.

Another and maybe simpler word for this is *patience*. Patience means understanding that you cannot possibly heal everything at once. But, if you stay sober and do the best you can in each moment, you can and will eventually get to a different place. Time itself is a healer.

Pushing off from here is not absolution from your mistakes; it is a posture of possibility instead of despair. It is an understanding that with time and action, you can and will make reparations and move into a place of being okay. Even great. I eventually had the capacity to deal with the piles of destruction, and so will you, but it couldn't happen then for me, and it can't all happen for you today.

And then there is faith, which is perhaps the most important sentiment of all here. I haven't talked about God yet, and if these two words — *faith* and *God* — make you flinch or shut down, replace them with whatever words feel all right to you. If you can't think of anything, *wonder* is a great word: just think about wonder.

What I mean by faith is simply this: when you enter into an unknown place, one where you haven't yet developed the skills to operate — and especially one where you don't even *want* to be — you have to rely on some idea that you will be carried through it and that it will be better.

Often, for me, faith simply meant deciding to trust the people who had gone before me. Like the women and men whose books I had read: Mary Karr, Anne Lamott, Caroline Knapp, Stephen King...surely they couldn't all just be full of shit, right? I had faith in that.

Same for the people in AA meetings, for that woman. I had to believe they weren't idiots, or lying, or drastically less complicated than I was. I had to believe that if I pushed off from here, I would eventually land somewhere better — somewhere I wanted to live.

I also had to believe I had in me the capacity for things I could not imagine in my mind. That somewhere within me there was a primal wisdom I could not possibly understand or access, but that not being able to didn't make it any less real. There was so much of life beyond my limited mental grasp — most of life, in fact. Breathing, for example. The impossible expanse of the ocean and the underworld it contains. Quantum physics. Animals. My daughter. So when I got really scared and thought a proud, dignified, peaceful sober life was beyond the pale of what was possible for me, I would say to myself, *I can't do this, but something inside me can.* I can't tell you how many times I've whispered those words in the dark.

Last, implied in the words *push off from here* is the idea that you must stop waiting. I had to stop *sort of* pushing off and instead go with both feet. As I learned in the year of trying and failing, there would be no day in the future when I'd be more willing, stronger, or more capable of pushing off from the past.

In bed this morning, warm, sober, and lying next to Alma, I feel the impossible: I am okay. She is okay. It is all okay.

Drop by drop, sobriety and time have healed my mama heart. All the breaking has only made it stronger. Back then, I figured I could maybe forgive myself for everything else I'd done, but not all that. Not her. *Never.*

That wasn't true. I have. I have, and I have, and I have... forgiven myself.

Because I pushed off.

And it will happen for you, too. However big your hole of regret is, and however badly it burns in there. Whatever you think the worst things you've done say about who you are, I can promise you this: you are wrong. But for now, just push off from here.

6

Hell Is Other People

*All improvements, transformations, achievements,
liberations; everything you want to change about yourself
and your life; everything you want to make happen, any obstacle
you want to overcome, any crisis you must survive — the
prerequisite is being able to allow yourself to feel whatever
it is you feel and not pretend to feel something you don't.*

— Augusten Burroughs, *This Is How*

I never noticed how *everywhere* drinking was until I stopped
doing it. I've heard other friends share this sentiment unre-
lated to long-term sobriety. When trying a Dry January or a
Sober October, for example, people will often comment on how
many times in a short thirty-one-day period they had to say no
to alcohol in order to abstain (to which I kind of want to say...
yeah, no shit).

Drinking, plans for drinking, casual references to drinking,
jokes about drinking, memes about drinking, advertisements
for drinking were everywhere — are everywhere. We live in a
culture that drinks by default, and although not everyone in my
life cared about drinking the way I did, most of them cared at
least a little.

For me, and most others, this is one of the hardest parts about getting sober or even imagining getting sober: the "other people" factor. Because not drinking alcohol isn't one of those things that generally goes under the radar. People notice. As it goes, alcohol is the only drug you have to explain *not* using. So there's the explaining part, which — whether you choose to do it or not — comes with all kinds of real or perceived judgment, pressure, and so on, and there's the "how do we do this thing now?" part, where you and the people in your circles try to navigate spending time together now that you're not drinking. Even if they know what's going on, they're often unsure how exactly to proceed. It's almost like showing up to Thanksgiving dinner with a bikini on. Even if some people aren't bothered by it, they're definitely going to notice and feel compelled to point it out. And there's no playbook. What's the etiquette? Offer a towel? Have everyone put on swimsuits? Act like nothing is different?

The thing is: It's about drinking, but it's about so much more than drinking. It's about feeling comfortable; it's about distancing ourselves from moments and people and feelings that we don't want to experience, and bringing closer the ones that we do; it's about self-medication; it's about belonging; it's about taking a little edge off a thousand kinds of discomfort; it's about status and appearance and sophistication; it's about sex and desire; it's about filling in the spaces we don't know how to otherwise fill. It's about having something to do with your damn hands. So when you, a newly sober person, walk into a room or sit at a dinner table, you are not just carrying in your own story; you are shining lots of little mirrors onto other people's stories, too. Sometimes, this causes a fleeting blip, a tiny disturbance, felt mostly by you. And sometimes, it sends shock waves.

A couple of months into my continuous sobriety, my mom had a dinner party. She lived one town away from me then, and Derek lived in San Antonio at the time — where she eventually joined him. He was in town that weekend, and they were having a small gathering of people.

For five years, Mom and I were neighbors on the north shore of Boston. Even before that she was close by, too. We saw each other once or twice a week, for dinner or to do something with Alma. She was always part of my friend gatherings. Holidays. Dinners out in the city. In the newer days of my separation from Jake, I would often leave Alma with her on weekend nights so I could go out. More often than I care to admit.

To add to her wonderful qualities, she is an incredible cook. Entertaining is one of her superpowers. When I was growing up, there was always a steady stream of friends and family passing through our doors, and the kitchen is where she works her magic. She is the consummate host, charming and funny and generous, and always has the wine and food flowing.

The food I was raised on was exceptional. She learned from the best: my grandparents, who were Italian immigrants. They made glorious, simple things: homemade sausage; piles of spaghetti and meatballs; split-pea soup with the ham bone in; the perfect Bolognese (add nutmeg); garlicky, peppery *aglio e olio*; tiramisu with sweetened mascarpone; cannoli with candied fruit.

What can I get you to drink?

This was always the first question you were asked as a guest in our home. I didn't think much of it until later. It was nice, mostly. Adults drank alcohol. And when you grew up, you could drink, too. Only later, after I'd spent significant time with other families and in other homes — like my husband's, for example — did I realize there were families who didn't roll this way. In my family, the drinks flowed a little more freely and often than in most.

When my mom and I spent time together as adults, we usually had wine. It seems unfair to her to say she was among my leading drinking pals because it sounds implicating of her, but that's the truth. She never encouraged me to go too far, but she never discouraged the drinking, either. I think at some point we both found it a little easier to be with each other with the softening of some wine.

She wasn't good at talking about things, and neither was I. Wine helped that, as it does — filling in the empty spaces you don't know how to fill. The truth was, I had grown resentful of her without knowing it, both for things she'd done and for things she hadn't. A wedge grew between us, and she responded by becoming more careful with me. I responded by becoming more guarded.

Wine helped with all of it.

It smoothed out the rocky rivers of our interiors — or at least it did mine. It allowed me to be around her, which I needed, and also not be *too* with her — the alcohol created a buffer, a chemical distancing — which I also needed.

Then, of course, we hit the wall. I stopped. She didn't.

Early into my attempts at sobriety, we went on a walk one Saturday afternoon. It was spring, and the weather was unseasonably warm. You could hear birds chirping as we circled the harbor. She asked how I was doing, and I coughed on the feeling of overwhelm that was always at the back of my throat, threatening to crash over me. What was I supposed to say? I was starving for a witness, but I couldn't take any platitudes.

"I'm doing okay. I mean, I'm doing it."

My eyes stayed fixed on our sneakers meeting the sidewalk. After a moment, I said, "But it's really hard."

"Of course it is, honey. Of course it is." Her response came too quickly, and was too light. I was overcome with an electric anger, an impulse to snap back at her and scream.

You don't fucking know, I wanted to say. *Don't act like you know. Nothing has changed for you.*

Instead I kept walking.

I wanted her to understand more but couldn't let her in. This was the constant bind I found myself in when I had tried to talk about it with anyone who was close to me then. But with her, it was especially hard.

Since my marriage had started to fall apart a couple of years before, I'd stopped being able to talk to her. The harder she tried, the more distant I became. Her vulnerability and emotionality repelled me; it often filled me with a hot rage I didn't understand. I couldn't really see this or understand it until years later — I'd always thought it was my dad I had the issues with — but I finally came to see, much later in sobriety, that I resented my mom because I simply could not separate her mistakes from my own; I rejected what I perceived to be a gross weakness in her, especially when it came to men, because I did not want to see the same in myself.

Plus, she had a way of slapping sunshine on complicated things, which I found infuriating. It was well-intentioned, of course, but it sometimes made me want to throw things.

"Who cares if you don't drink, honey? There are a lot of people who don't drink."

I think she was trying to fill the space. Something I'd tried to do a hundred times and something so many people tried to do with me. She wanted to make it feel better. But it did not feel better. It felt so much worse than she could possibly know. But I nodded and pretended to agree.

The truth was, we *didn't* know a lot of people who didn't drink. We'd made jokes about not trusting people who didn't drink. Everyone we knew liked to drink. Everyone we *liked* liked to drink. What was I supposed to do with that?

"One of Susan's friends, Cynthia — do you know her?" She kept going, filling the silence. "She came to our office party the other day, and she doesn't drink. Neither does her partner."

Mom went on with the story. It wasn't helping. I was becoming even more enraged. I could feel my face getting hotter and hotter, and a sharp pressure radiating in my chest.

"It'll take time," I said, closing the subject.

Since my brother's wedding, there had been an elephant in the room: when we were together, would my mom drink, or not? It wasn't just a question for her — I wondered this with everyone whom I drank with in the past — but with family, it was especially tricky.

The first couple of times, she did, though I wasn't technically there. For example, she'd come to my place to watch Alma a few Monday nights because I had to attend an alcohol-awareness class — a requirement for the DUI I'd gotten earlier in the year. When I returned home at 9 PM, there would be an empty wineglass in the sink, or I'd see a half-full bottle in her bag.

We could have talked about it, but I didn't know how.

Then one night there was a small dinner party at her house. Calling it a party was a stretch, but it might as well have been a black-tie gala at the Museum of Fine Arts, for even the idea of anything social at that point spun me out. Life itself had become a constant affront, a battleground I had to maneuver through so carefully, so as not to fall back into drinking or despair. Being anywhere where people were drinking was like sitting in the same room with the lover I still adored but who no longer loved me and watching him fall for someone else. It was torture.

But it was the weekend, and they stretched on so long now. Alma couldn't sit still for long, and going to Mom's house would break up the day. It took care of dinner. The food would be good. It gave me a small reprieve from single parenting. They wanted us to come. *What's the big deal, Laura?* was the constant refrain in my mind then, about every basic social engagement. *Just go.* And so, exhausted by my own inner dialogue, I went.

When we arrived, only my mom and Derek were there. I immediately noticed Derek had a drink in hand, but my mom didn't have anything. *Huh.*

Her friends arrived; we sat around the table snacking on antipasto. Alma kept asking for more Marcona almonds and "little pickles" — cornichons — her favorites. I got myself a seltzer from the cabinet. Mom served red wine to her friends. We chatted, and when Alma predictably grew tired of the adult talk, she asked to go watch a show on Nonna's iPad in the bedroom. I set it up and lingered on the bed with her for a while, messing around on my phone, wishing I could just stay in there and fall asleep. Eventually, I returned to the grown-ups and rejoined the conversation.

I don't remember what was served; I don't even remember the names or faces of her friends. But I did notice with precise clarity that my mom's wineglass stayed empty throughout dinner. I noticed every refill the other adults had, every time a new bottle was opened, every trip they made to the kitchen to refill ice cubes and refresh a drink.

We ate dinner. I fixed a plate for Alma, and she ate some of it. We might have had dessert. I can't remember. What I remember is how everyone lingered around the table, as people do, as I had always liked to do. I remember that I found myself suddenly bone-tired, out of words, out of will. I went back to the bedroom to visit Alma. "Are you ready to go home, sweetie?" I was so grateful to have a small child as an excuse to leave when it would otherwise be odd to bolt so quickly after dinner. It wasn't even eight o'clock yet.

I announced we were going to go, my mom packed us some food to take home, and we got our coats on, said goodbyes, and left.

My mom's building had an elevator, and Alma always wanted to race me to it, summon it to our floor, press the close-doors button, then press the right button to take us up to Mom's floor or down to the lobby. As we were waiting for the elevator doors to open, I fished for my car keys in my purse and realized I'd left them at my mom's. We backtracked through the hallway, and I knocked on the door, but the lock hadn't latched, so we popped back inside.

"Forgot my keys!" I said as I walked in, surprising them.

Right away I noticed my mom was pouring herself a glass of wine from a bottle that wasn't open when I left. Freshly corked. I spotted my keys in the kitchen, scooped them up, and with a laugh from everyone, announced my leaving again "for real this time!"

On the way back to the elevator, tears sprang into my eyes, and a knot of something thick and acidic formed in my throat.

That fast. Mere seconds after I left.

In the elevator, Alma noticed I was crying. "What's wrong, Mama?" she asked, confused.

We rode down. *Beep...beep...beep...ding!* the elevator said, before the doors opened.

"Nothing, baby. I'm just tired."

The moment cut through me in so many ways.

First, this was the thought I couldn't erase from my mind, the one that played on repeat over and over again: *She had been waiting for me to leave.* My own mom — even as she wanted me there, and I knew she honestly did — was waiting for me to leave. So she could drink wine, with everyone else.

How long had she been pining for that wine?

And if my own mom felt that way, if she scrambled for the wine and had a glass in hand within thirty seconds of me walking out the door, how badly did other people — people who were supposedly, by definition, less invested in my well-being — want me to leave, too?

I know, of course, that there are other explanations. She was waiting because she loved me and wanted to respect me. She was actually *supporting* me. The wine wasn't as big a deal to her as it is to me, and I was projecting my experience onto her.

But still. *Still.*

It confirmed my worst fears, fears I had up to that point muzzled lest they crush me: I was a burden. A buzzkill. Having alcohol with dinner (or whenever) was important. Preferred. A better time. A better life. And having me around was an impediment to *preferred* and *better.* I was an outsider, on the outside now, in this way, forever.

On the drive back home, I thought of what she'd said on our walk that one day: "Who cares if you don't drink, honey?"

Well. Apparently you *do.*

I wanted to bash my fists into the steering wheel. Fuck her for pretending that it was no big deal, that it didn't matter. Fuck her for pretending that "a lot of people don't drink" when she was counting down the seconds until I walked out the door.

In addition to what felt like my worst nightmare realized, there was also just the regular old bloody heartbreak.

I *missed* drinking.

I couldn't believe I would never drink another glass of red wine with my mom, or anyone, ever again. Not in the way I once had. I would never be able to sit there and slip into the easy flow of a dinner party buoyed by the flow of drinks among company. How was this entire part of life just *gone*?

And then, there was the recoil of shame for feeling all this shit in the first place. To miss something that was so clearly killing me felt dumb and immature. I mean, I had done this to myself. It wasn't my mom's fault or anyone else's that I had a problem. What did I *really* want her — or anyone else — to do? Would I prefer that she carry on as usual and drink in front of me like nothing was different, or did I want her to change her behavior for my sake, like she did that night, if she didn't really want to? The thought of other people doing that made me feel heavy and despondent and humiliated.

There was no better option, no softer place. Both ways ached.

I drove the few miles home that night imagining what everyone else in my world was likely doing on a Saturday night at eight o'clock. My world had become very small. I had only a few local connections who were more acquaintances than friends: parents of Alma's friends from preschool, a couple of neighbors, students from the yoga class I taught — no one I would consider calling or texting on a weekend.

My close friends had already been scattered for a couple of years by then — a natural result of people getting married and starting families of their own. But I had also distanced myself from many of them through the divorce, or they had distanced themselves from me, as they had been *our* friends: me and Jake's, as a couple. He might be out with them right now, somewhere in the city. Or maybe on a date. With a few exceptions, most had fallen on the side of allying with him after the divorce. He was the injured party. I had largely been a horrible partner, at least in the later years of our relationship. In his angriest moments he exposed the details of my mistakes. I didn't blame him. I accepted whatever had come as a result as fair payment for shitting all over his dreams.

For so long, my drinking had provided a rip cord in moments just like those — when the fear crept in too close, when I felt alone or rejected, when I had a truth I wasn't sure how to say. Alcohol was a way to create instant distance or intimacy, indifference or bravado, to propel myself into incapacitation or chaos.

And now. Now, there was just the chaos with no escape. Sometimes, it vibrated at a low-level, ominous hum. And sometimes, like that night, it crashed in battering waves, hammering.

An emptiness.

A crushing emptiness.

So much space.

The most painful thought blistered and burst inside me: *You don't belong to anyone. Anywhere.*

Driving home, I wanted to scream at the black of night. Alma drifted to sleep in her car seat, and I wanted to cave into myself and disappear. I wanted to run my fingers through my hair and pull fistfuls out of my head. I wanted everything to be different.

The reality of my day-to-day was this: despite my continual attempts at sobriety, a booze cart circulated around the office every Thursday at 3 PM on the dot, offering a selection of wine and beer for anyone interested. This was actually quite tame in comparison to my prior offices, where we had literal bars with always-full kegs of craft beer installed, liquid lunches were frequent, and drinking at your desk in the late afternoon was perfectly normal on any day, not just on Thursday. On the way home from work, I passed by dozens of bars, restaurants, and liquor stores — most of which held a story or a memory for me. My friends were always cooking up something that involved drinking: a birthday outing, a barbecue, a Tuesday night out after work. Invites rolled in constantly from former grad-school or work colleagues for marathon fund-raisers, promotion celebrations, or someone leaving for a new job or a new city. Weekend playdates with kids included beverages, at least with the crew I hung with. Entertaining clients or partners for lunch always involved at least a couple of drinks, and when I traveled to meet with clients, drinks were an expected and anticipated part of the experience.

So when it came to getting sober, the people closest to me supported me in theory, but they didn't really get it. They didn't know how to talk about it, or what to do exactly, any more than I did. No one had gone through this themselves, so all they knew was what most of society knows, which can be summed up like this: There is a small percentage of people who have a problem with drinking or drugs, and when they "hit bottom," they go to AA meetings, where they "do the steps" and "collect chips" and, hopefully, get better. Everyone else is good to go.

Even people I've talked to in recent years about the kind of sober experiments I mentioned earlier — people who tried a Sober October or a Dry January but wouldn't consider themselves problematic drinkers — were surprised by how often they found themselves turning down the opportunity to drink while abstaining. They hadn't realized how omnipresent alcohol was until they were consciously saying no to it, and were amazed by the feelings and questions not drinking brought up in them and from others.

My instinct for many months was to go it alone, to take up as little space as possible and get sober in the background of my life, but that required — well, it required erasing myself completely. And though I tried (oh, how I tried) to put on a good face and keep things as they were before, to show everyone just how *chill* I was with the whole thing, it didn't work. I just suffered more.

So, what do we do about this? The harsh reality is that life always keeps going. Whether it's sobriety, weight loss, love, pregnancy, health, your work, or something else, it's a cruel fact: no matter what you have to face, life doesn't stop and wait for you to get comfortable first.

It just goes.

The sun comes up. People throw parties and get promoted. Holidays show up just like they did the year before. Babies are born, and meals are made and the dishes pile up in the sink, again and again. And you? Either you change, or you don't.

I can't tell you what you should do, and I can't give you a list of neatly ordered advice and promise it will help. What I can do is the only thing I know how to do, which is to tell you what I did, and promise you it did help me. Things did eventually feel better. My life today is nothing like my life back then.

Just yesterday, I woke at 4:30 AM and wrote an entire three-thousand-word chapter of this book in two hours. I called my friend to say, "I think I'm done writing for the day, maybe?" And she said, "I think you are."

Then I worked with the students in the course I'm teaching, took a glorious nap where I dreamed about hanging out with Joe Rogan, got a ninety-minute massage, ate some soup and had a cup of coffee with the senior citizens at Panera, created my first original meme, got cat food, got my eyebrows waxed, went and bought some new underwear and pajamas because mine are sad, came home and Marie Kondo'd my whole closet, folded all my laundry while watching *Schitt's Creek*, picked up Alma from play practice, went and got some dinner, came home, came up with a costume/hair plan for her school dance Friday, washed and folded new clothes, organized my snack bins, and cleaned out the kitty litter. All the while thinking, *I am the* luckiest *goddamn person in the world.*

I often think of a quote by Khalil Gibran: "The deeper that sorrow carves into your being, the more joy you can contain." Yes, this is the shape of me today.

The first big step in getting there was that when it came to situations like the one at my mom's that night, I finally stopped pretending that I felt differently than I did. I'd spent my whole life trying to bypass anger, rejection, and weakness. I'd created an entire persona in order to avoid feeling those things.

I remember the first time I caught myself doing this. Early

on in sobriety, I was talking to Holly on the phone while walking to the train after work. I was sighing into the phone, exas-
perated and near tears, because it literally hurt my body to walk
through the five o'clock hour in Boston sometimes, knowing
that this time of day would never again mean I was going to slip
into the ease of drinking. Even if I did decide to drink again, it
would never be with the same ignorance I once had. She asked
me a question that made me stop, midstride. "Wait, Laura. Do
you *miss* drinking?" I thought she was joking, but she wasn't.

I started to do the thing I had been doing, which was to bypass my actual feelings and say the thing I knew I was supposed
to say: the more spiritual thing, the thing I thought she wanted
to hear. Something like, *Well, I mean, no — of course not. I know
it's not what's best for me. It's just some lesser part of me that thinks
it misses it. I'm fine.* But I stopped myself. I breathed.

Finally, I said, "Yes, I fucking miss it. I miss it every day. All
the time."

There it was.

Everything in me wanted to take it back, or to explain more,
or to qualify it with some kind of higher wisdom.

But another thing happened inside me then, too.

I felt a burst of expansion, like a pressure valve had been released.

Most of my life up to that point had been a series of small or
large acts of pretending, which made the ground I was standing
on shaky and unstable. I was never going to feel whole standing
on that ground, even when it appeared to be attractive, solid,
and right, because it was built on falsities and my soul knew it.

One Sunday afternoon in the fall of 2013, Jake had come to pick
up Alma, and I was left with the terrifying empty space of an

open, childless sunny afternoon — a time when I would have typically slid right into plans at a restaurant or bar with friends or a date, or even thrown myself a little wine party at home and trailed off into a comfortable numbness. I instead sat there in my big red chair. Sober.

I looked around at the empty, cavernous room; I still hadn't filled it with more furniture since Jake moved out the year before. And I wailed. I sobbed and screamed, and it echoed off the walls and the hardwood floors. I scared my dog. She hid behind the couch.

When I was done, I grabbed a pen and a piece of paper and furiously wrote everything down. It was maybe the first honest thing I'd ever written. I set down all the ugly words and the humiliating thoughts and the messiness of what I hadn't been able to admit to myself yet. Things like "no one will ever love me" and "what if I'm boring?" and "I hate my mom and everyone else in my family who doesn't have a fucking 'problem' — fuck them ALL" and "my heart is broken."

This is part of what I wrote that day:

I am the saddest girl in the world. Time isn't moving. I'm aware of every goddamn thing I'm doing and not doing.

Here I am, driving my daughter home from school, not going to get wine.

Here I am, taking a walk to the park, not drinking.

Here I am, cooking dinner, without wine.

Here I am, riding the train home.

Here I am, sitting in a meeting.

Here I am, running — drinking coffee — talking to a coworker — eating lunch — sending a text — watching *House of Cards*.

Here I am, coming out of my skin.

Two years later, I would look back on those words and use them to write an essay called "The Girl in the Big Red Chair." It would become my first published essay, in *Elephant Journal*, and the way a lot of people would first find me and my writing. Which in some way has led me to write these words now, in my first book, which you're reading. All because I finally admitted what was true: I was in hell, and I hated that other people could drink and I couldn't.

The truth is alchemical. It transmutes the bitterness of pain and dishonesty and shame into something else, something we can actually live in and stand on. You will hear me talk about telling the truth throughout this book, over and over again, because it is that important. It is also difficult to do because — for many of us — it's in conflict with how we've learned to get our needs met.

But the first step here is to be real with yourself. You don't have to show your guts to anyone else, not yet. Acknowledge the truth of how you feel about the thing you are going through, and *leave nothing unsaid*. Whisper it into the dark, say it in a prayer, write it down on paper — whatever. Just get it out of your body. That's what I did that day, and it started to change everything. Today can be the day you do the same.

The second thing that really helped was that I tapped out of the hell that is other people drinking. As in, I just stopped going to places where I knew it would be around. Period. Until I felt differently (without believing that I ever really would). No matter how big a deal the thing was to me or anyone else, I said no. Weddings. Showers. Client dinners. Client lunches. Work trips. Dates. Happy hours. Birthdays. Playdates. I bowed out of anything that felt like it was an affront to what I needed most, which was safety and space and the simplicity of just being without having to fight so hard against the tide. This can be incredibly hard and painful at first because it feels like social suicide, but with each *no* my spirit exhaled a deep, profound, long-awaited *thank you*.

I was giving myself a chance.

I remember standing at my desk one morning, a few months into trying for sobriety, when I got a text from my friend Kate. I'd just seen a post on Facebook from our mutual friends — photos from a party over the weekend I didn't know about. Seeing the pictures gutted me: both that I didn't know it had happened and that even if I had known about it and been included, I likely wouldn't have gone. Kate and I had been friends for fifteen years, roommates for a long stretch of that time, and she, more than any of my friends, had witnessed the worst of me and my drinking.

In our conversation, she'd simply asked how I was doing. She was traveling across India and Thailand and South Africa at the time, so our typically daily check-ins had become far less frequent.

I stared at her simple question, wrapped so neatly in a text bubble, illuminated on my phone screen.

How are you doing?

I couldn't bring myself to answer in a way I typically would have — in the way I wanted to answer — or even just to offer a banal "Doing okay" or "I'm good" that would have moved us along to exchanging updates or stories.

Shitty, I replied, out of character.

:(I'm sorry, peach, she said.

I explained to her what I'd seen on Facebook. She tried to encourage me, letting me know that people didn't know what to do, and I understood that — I did — but it didn't change the fact that it felt like shit. Because, again, I didn't belong there right now, but I also didn't belong or want to be anywhere else. I was in a stalemate.

What can I do? she asked after I had been silent for a while.

I thought about it. I wished I knew of something.

I don't know. I cried as I hit "send."

Do you want to be invited to things? It's hard to tell.

I thought some more.

I don't know. I said it again. It was the only thing that was true: I just didn't know what she or anyone else could do, or what I wanted them to, or what I would feel like in five seconds.

OK. Well, when you do, let me know. Love you.

I love you too.

I sat with that conversation for a while. As someone who rarely ever says "I don't know," it felt horribly bare — and humiliating? — to say it. But there was some suspicious freedom in it. Not the kind of freedom that feels invigorating and sweet, like a day off work at the beach, but like taking off shoes that are way too tight.

It was disorienting and scary to be in this messy, in-between place of not belonging and not knowing what to do to make it better, but admitting that I didn't know brought the tiniest sliver of relief. Sometimes it was totally fine when other people were drinking around me! Sometimes even the thought of it sent me into a fit of rage! Sometimes I was fine! Sometimes I was a puddle! Yes, I wanted to be invited! No, I didn't want the stress of saying no!

It made no sense. I made no sense. None of this made any sense. I didn't know what to do, and maybe that was just fine.

Maybe I could just figure out what was going to work as I went along. Maybe I could ask for what I needed in that moment, even if it was something different from what I'd needed the moment before.

This is what I started to do and what I suggest you do, too. Tell people you have no idea what they can do to help, but to keep asking, please — until you tell them to stop asking, of course — and that if you can think of something in the moment, you'll tell them, and if you can't, you'll tell them that, too.

Tell them you have no answers right now, only questions. Tell them you never know if it's going to be hard to be around the drinking, and that sometimes you may just have to say no over and over again, but to please keep inviting you to things, until you are able to say yes again — but, of course, maybe you won't ever say yes again. More than anything, just give yourself permission to tell the truth. Even when it doesn't make sense. Even when it makes you feel like the high-maintenance person you've never wanted to be. Not everyone will get this, but the important people will, and you only need one or two in your corner. It is so helpful to have space to figure things out and to stop pretending like any of us knows what to do, because we almost never do.

Today, I don't have to think about these things before I go places. I don't have to wonder about the presence of alcohol or people drinking it and how it might wreak havoc on my psyche. I don't have to assess the risk of how much I might feel like drinking or whether or not by saying yes or no I will be risking relationships or connections. It changed, but only because I let myself be messy until I wasn't so messy anymore.

I will never forget the first time I went to a sober party. I have to admit, the thought of it was totally depressing and even kind of embarrassing. Like, what were we doing to *do*? Crafts? Cards? Trivia? What would we talk about? What would we do with our hands? Do people dress the same way when they go to a sober party as they do when they're going out to... *not* be sober?

It wasn't the first one I'd been invited to, but it was the first time I felt comfortable enough to show up. It was at a woman's apartment in Jamaica Plain, a far-off corner of Boston and an hour away from my house in the burbs. But I trekked back in after coming home from work to let my dog out, arriving strategically after my sponsor had already texted me to tell me she was there so I knew I'd see at least one familiar face when I walked in. When I got there, it took everything I had just to keep from turning around and running back to my car. The place was packed! And so loud! There was music playing and food all over: pizzas, appetizers, chips and salsa, chips and dip, chips of all kinds. Cookies. Brownies. Bags of candy. And seltzer. Boxes and boxes of seltzer! Everyone must have brought their own case, there was so much goddamn seltzer.

I made a beeline for a package of Oreos and then frantically scanned the room for my sponsor, who was standing way in the back, engrossed in a conversation with a group of women. When was the last time I'd walked into a house party knowing only one person? Literally never.

I started to make my way over to her — maybe to tell her I

had to leave, that something came up with Alma — when someone grabbed my arm.

"Laura!" a man threw his arms up. A guy I'd met a bunch of times at meetings but whose name I couldn't remember was suddenly right in front of me; he hugged me, then introduced me to the other people he was standing with. I squeezed the Oreos in my hand.

They resumed whatever they'd been talking about before, and I joined in where I could, amazed by how hard everyone was laughing.

The whole room was an eruption of laughter. *Who knew?*

I can't say it was the easiest social experience. I was awkward and felt like the part of my brain that knew how to converse had been lopped off and left in my car.

I spoke out of turn. I laughed too loud at inappropriate times. I drank about sixty-four seltzers and made myself sick with candy. But I remember at one point going to the bathroom and, while folding up toilet paper in my hand, noticing a lack of...something. As weird and awkward and confusing as it was to be in this place not knowing anyone, socializing without drinking, and feeling like I couldn't string sentences together very well, I also didn't feel hypervigilant like I did around alcohol. The pressure just wasn't there. To have it or not have it, or watch people having it without trying to act like I didn't notice, or to be around it.

It was like walking into a bar for the first time in Boston after they passed the no-smoking law in 2004. I hadn't noticed how suffocating the air had been before, not until all that smoke was simply gone.

And, of course, everyone at that party knew each other without knowing each other. We all knew, by virtue of the fact that we were there, more than most people will ever know about one another. We were united by this bizarre, common struggle, and it wasn't even something that had to be said out loud — most of the conversations didn't touch on drinking or sobriety at all — but if you did want to talk about it, you would be met exactly where you were. We all got it.

I fought this hard, and maybe you're fighting it, too. I didn't want to find new people. I didn't think they would measure up at all. I didn't believe I needed it.

I was, of course, very wrong.

One stranger who understands your experience exactly will do for you what hundreds of close friends and family who don't understand cannot. It is the necessary palliative for the pain of stretching into change. It is the cool glass of water in hell.

7

The Pregnancy Principle

Manifestation requires an acceptance of limitation.
A boundary allows us to contain,
and thus to collect and build.

— ANODEA JUDITH, *Eastern Body, Western Mind*

At thirty I was the first of my friends to have a baby, and at first, I tried to go to parties and dinners and such, to show I wasn't going to lose myself just because I was growing a human inside me. My tendency for people-pleasing and FOMO — fear of missing out — was as sky-high then as it had ever been in my life, and I also felt like I had something to prove. I didn't want to lose my connection to my friends and the life I'd had prepregnancy, and I wanted to show myself that nothing would change. I felt anxious if I bowed out of things or didn't return texts and calls, like people were going to forget about me.

But I also just couldn't push through how I felt, physically. I was green for the first half of my pregnancy. Morning sickness, all day. The only moments I enjoyed were unconscious ones, because while asleep, I had a reprieve from the *I'm going to throw up again any second now* sensation that churned in my stomach constantly.

In hindsight, I can see this so clearly as a screaming indication of my inability to just be with myself. Without constantly being in motion, making plans, finding validation from the outside world, and, of course, drinking, I was thoroughly uncomfortable and on edge.

I complained to Kacey about how I felt, and she said something that stayed with me for a long time. She said, "Girl, this time *has* to be about you and the baby. You can either fight that or go with it, but fighting will only make you suffer more. Do exactly what you need to do. No one is going to argue with a pregnant woman."

For some reason, her words touched down. Throwing up every couple of hours certainly helped force the issue, but even so, I was able to internalize what she said and actually relax into it. When I started saying no to almost anything extra and just flowing with what my body needed in the moment, I felt such tidal relief. It was as if I'd unlocked some magical hidden secret of the universe. My body practically wept.

I wondered how many things I did every day that I didn't really, actually want to do. I wondered how long I had been hurtling forward unconsciously, propelled by the fear of what might happen if I stopped.

I worked full-time during my pregnancy. We still had to pay bills, run errands, navigate family, friends, in-laws, a new mortgage we could barely afford, one income while Jake was finishing grad school, and other life stuff. But for the most part, I let the noise fall away. I focused on my body. I let Jake take care of a lot. I stayed in bed many weekends, all weekend, reading and listening to Pema Chödrön and reading Anne Lamott. I didn't shower much, but when I did, they were long, hot, luxurious affairs. I ate a lot of Sour Patch Kids and Eggo waffles slathered with butter. I started toying with writing a little. I completed a two-hundred-hour yoga teacher training, and the last fifty hours or so were mostly spent lying on my side letting one of the other students pet my head.

If we had company in our home, I ducked out when I got tired and went to sleep. Same deal if we were at someone else's place. It was the kindest I'd ever treated myself, and although there was still a decent amount of anxiety upstairs, I let a lot of stuff just go.

I became, in essence, unapologetically selfish with my energy and time. And Kacey was right — no one questioned me or pushed back. Because no one is confused about the importance of being pregnant.

In the first year of trying to get sober, I was tired all the time. Not the adrenaline-fueled tired I used to feel when I was still drinking but something more weighted and bone level, like the flu. I drank more coffee. I practiced Kapalabhati breathing (a rapid inhale and exhale breath technique I learned from yoga). It made me look and sound like I might be possessed, but I didn't care — I still did this, even on the train to and from work and in bathroom stalls at the office, just to try to make it through my next meeting or conference call. More than once, I called in sick to work because I simply could not drag my body there.

I ran. I bought a big juicer that took up half my kitchen counter and made fresh, life-giving juices. I took vitamins. I slept eight, ten, twelve hours a night. I spent time turning my face toward the sun. And although I would have occasional bursts of almost manic energy, in which I woke up at 4 AM and wrote a five-thousand-word blog post, or scrubbed my entire house floor to ceiling, or ran seven miles, mostly I felt like I was slogging through mud.

I found this to be so frustrating and unfair, because it seemed like now that I wasn't drowning myself in wine every night, life should automatically be...easier. Better. My body should feel like a demigod's. I wanted the energy to do all the things lighting up my brain: write more, start a podcast, start my book, fix up my apartment, clean my car, paint my bedroom, find a boyfriend, *live* — but most days, I could barely make it through the afternoon without crying.

Several times, I experienced déjà vu back to my pregnancy — the only other time I'd felt such bone-level fatigue. And that's what got me started thinking about Kacey's words. Then one evening on the drive home from work, as I was blasting both the AC and music just to stay awake, an entire theory downloaded into my brain.

The theory was this: *this* isn't actually any different from being pregnant.

I mean, I know it is. But it also isn't.

You don't have to be a woman or a mother to get this, and in fact, you'll get it if you've ever felt the kind of daunting exhaustion I'm talking about — no matter what it was related to. I call this the Pregnancy Principle. It goes something like this:

The Pregnancy Principle

1. You are building a new life.
2. The new life you are building comes first, period.
3. Anything or anyone that doesn't support the new life goes.
4. Nothing trumps the process.

You Are Building a New Life

Let's talk for a minute first about building a new life. This is not the same as, say, cleaning out your closet, learning how to knit, or starting CrossFit. This isn't just making a self-improvement or productivity tweak so your life can be 20 percent more organized and interesting, or so you can get a great-looking ass or earn $15,000 more a year; I'm talking about the kind of change that requires death and rebirth.

Maybe you're trying to get sober. Or maybe you're at the end of a relationship, or someone you love has passed, or you're making a huge professional leap, or a season of your life is coming to an end or already has. Whether it's something that you've chosen or something that has befallen you, the result is the same: you are going to have to build a new way of being. That can sound clear and linear, like something that can be project-managed, but real transformation doesn't work that way. My friend Lisa says, "Getting sober ain't like other task-oriented activities, sweetie," and this is hilariously, and unfortunately, true. It's bigger. Wider. Deeper. Entirely engrossing. Otherworldly, even.

In every big transition of my life — pregnancy, becoming a mother, marriage, divorce, and especially getting sober — I have been gobsmacked by the messiness and difficulty of it all. It can feel like the most basic tasks, things you have been doing since childhood — taking a shower, brushing your teeth, feeding yourself — are new again and near impossible. Time slows. Axioms you've understood and relied on all your life fall away. There is a profound and complete dislocation from the very center of things, as if gravity itself has relocated.

There's a term for these phases of life in biblical and psychological terms: *liminal space*. *Limen* is a Latin word that means "threshold." It is the time between the "what was" and the "next," a place of transition, waiting, and not knowing. Generally, we resist and wish like hell against these times, but for me, learning that it was an actual spiritual thing *defined* by groundlessness helped a lot. In *Everything Belongs*, author and theologian Richard Rohr describes liminal space as the place "where we are betwixt and between. There, the old world is left behind, but we're not sure of the new one yet.... Get there often and stay as long as you can by whatever means possible." He says, "If we don't find liminal space in our lives, we start idolizing normalcy."

And yet, we always think it should be easier. Faster. Less gnarly.

The Instagram culture we live in doesn't help. All the sparkly, shiny images of people #livingtheirbestlife #soberAF can make it look like sobriety, or any other significant transformation, is an instant reality. We don't see the daily fight — the thousands of tedious, unsexy steps — it takes, day after day, to really heal and become new.

My friend Janet said to me many times early on, when I would come to her vexed, once again, by the sheer difficulty of getting through a single day without drinking, "Girl, don't forget that you are saving your life — it should be hard." I thought that sounded rather dramatic. But, of course, she was right. I was saving my damn life. I was building a new life. It was never, will never, be anything less than that.

It doesn't matter if you haven't edged as close to disaster as I did. It doesn't matter if no one has ever commented on your drinking or no one believes you when you say you have a problem. As they say, it doesn't matter how much you drink, or how often, but what happens to you when you do. If something is keeping you from being fully present and showing up in your life the way you want, then deciding to change that thing is an actual matter of life and death, you know? It's the difference between existing and actually living.

Doesn't it make sense that, as with a pregnancy, you're going to have to fight like hell to bring this new life into the world?

If you are doing anything new, you are building a new life. Nothing less. New life does not burst forth fully formed on day one; it is at first a pink, tender thing that requires attention, vigilance, and respect. It takes time and tending to get big enough and strong enough to exist on its own. I really want you to hear that.

Which leads me to...

The New Life You Are Building Comes First, Period

I know this is something you hear all the time. *Put your own oxygen mask on first. Take care of* you.

It's easy to hear this and nod and say you get it and you're *trying*, but if you're anything like me, you don't actually have a clue what it means to operate this way, because either:

a. you're an award-winning codependent who can't distinguish your needs from others';
b. you are delusional about who and what actually support your well-being versus what depletes it; or
c. you drastically underestimate what it takes to actually change.

I was a big, fat *raise-your-hand to all three*!

Women, especially, have a long list of very good reasons why they simply can't put themselves first: the kids, the job, the partner, the bills, the birthday party, the house, the next holiday, and so forth, forever. To actually practice this feels radical and foreign and often plain wrong. We equate taking care of ourselves first with one of the evilest words in the English language, the *S* word: *Selfish*.

I could go on and on about the importance of putting sobriety first in the sense of priority, but the primary way I want you to look at this point is through the lens of permission. Permission to put sobriety first, *whatever that means*.

Not as in, permission to put sobriety first so long as it doesn't inconvenience others or make them uncomfortable. Not as in, permission to put sobriety first but only if people really understand what you're doing and support your choices. Not as in, permission to put sobriety first for a couple of weeks. I mean full permission, 110 percent permission, permission that feels like your needs are taking up *way* too much space, permission that feels rather dramatic. You know, like your life depends on it.

This is the thing: drinking is too easy. It's one of the easiest, everywhere-all-the-time and marketed-to-us-as-if-it's-the-duct-tape-of-life things people do in our culture. But if you're like me, it's as big as it gets. It almost killed me. And I needed the permission to treat it like that. So if you need the same, I'm giving it to you.

Generally speaking, pregnant women don't ask for permission to put the life growing inside them first. They are very clear about their priorities and what feels right and what doesn't, and they act accordingly — almost intuitively. They don't view taking care of the life inside them as selfish, only necessary.

What if you took the same approach to this new life you're growing?

Although both you and the outside world probably see getting sober differently from being pregnant, you don't have to, because I'm telling you: it's really not that different.

Anything or Anyone That Doesn't Support the New Life Goes

Before I was pregnant, I was regularly running five, six, seven miles a few times a week. I assumed I would just continue to run as my belly was growing. I mean, I saw women with protruding, round bellies zipping all over our neighborhood in South Boston all the time. But it took exactly one attempt at putting my feet to the pavement to know that it was not happening again.

Then there were the foods. A whole host of things, but particularly eggs — the sight of them, smell of them, thought of them — made me retch in the first eight months of my pregnancy, and then in the last month, I craved omelets. There are a hundred examples like this — shifts my body made intuitively or things I sensed weren't right for me. I didn't question it. I just stopped running. I avoided eggs, and then, later on, I ate omelets. You learn to listen to what your body is telling you and respect it. Almost worship it. Revere it. Because it is helping you, growing you, changing you, saving you. It is growing your new life.

One of my friends, at a few months sober, was stressing out about whether or not to serve alcohol to guests she was having over for dinner. This had been the norm in the past, of course, and she knew they would be expecting it. She didn't really want to serve it but felt obligated, or like she owed them an explanation if she didn't. Privately, she didn't even want to keep alcohol in the house at all, but since her husband drank, she felt like removing it all was a little unfair. She didn't want to impose her issues on him.

I got it. As I said, I grew up in a home where people were constantly flowing in and out, and the cocktails flowed, too. It was great fun. I liked being in a home that felt welcoming, warm: full of food, people, laughter, love.

No surprise, my own home mimicked this scene once I grew up. And when I was faced with the idea of sobriety, this picture was among the most painful to break. I didn't think a picture of entertaining even *existed* without wine painted into it. I couldn't imagine having others over and not extending that romantic age-old question *What can I get you to drink?* I couldn't imagine not sharing that ritual with others in my home. *Who would want to come over? Who would ever visit me again? What does this look like?* It broke my heart.

Eventually, I realized that the idea of keeping alcohol in my house or buying it for people when I had them over, or even *thinking* about any of that, jacked me up and spun me out. So I took the whole thing off the table altogether: not just alcohol in the house but having people over too.

Much later, when it felt right, I decided to have people over. It was a last-minute, casual get-together on Friday after work: a few friends in the neighborhood would bring their kids over; we'd order pizza; and they and Alma and I would head across the street to the beach afterward. I told the wives to bring beer or wine if they wanted, and when they showed up with wine, I did the math and realized I hadn't had alcohol in my house for ten months. Ten months before, I'd finally started respecting my own limits, even when they seemed over-the-top, overprotective, ridiculous. I'd finally stopped pretending I was at point C when I was at point A.

And guess what? I'd been sober for... ten months.

I told my friend to play out different scenarios in her head and see what felt the most right. To *her*, not her guests. This was a foreign concept to her, but I asked her to think about it as if she was pregnant and her friends wanted to bring a truckload of raw sushi over to share. Would she hem and haw about whether or not she was going to offend them by saying "Sorry, guys, I'm not eating raw fish while I'm growing a human," or would she just plan for something else?

This, of course, was about much deeper stuff, like the fear of social suicide and the shame of what it might mean if she told her friends she wasn't drinking, not to mention the hesitation to ask for what she needed in terms of support from her husband. But again, this part is specifically about permission and doing what someone who was putting their sobriety first would do. Thinking about it in those terms made things very clear: she didn't even want to have people over for dinner. She was only doing it because she didn't want to feel like her social life was going to die. She wanted to show her husband that life would still be fun — that *she* would still be fun! — even though she wasn't drinking anymore. She thought she had to make the whole thing easy and smooth for him, and everyone else.

She was putting *all* these things, without even realizing it, above her sobriety. Above this new little life growing inside her.

After our conversation, my friend worked up the courage to have one of the first honest conversations with her husband since she'd decided to get sober. It was scary and hard — these conversations almost always are; they're supposed to be — but then the most miraculous thing happened. Similar to when I started to say no to things in my pregnancy after my conversation with Kacey, she felt like she could finally breathe. She realized how much she had been pretending and how utterly exhausting it had been. Her husband was mostly supportive; although he could not totally understand how she felt, he was at least willing to try. He agreed to empty their bar for now, and that down the road they'd reevaluate what felt right.

It's important to add here that not every conversation goes

like this — not everyone in your life is going to care about what it is you want and need. But the most important part is that *you* see this thing you're doing as the most important thing in the world, and that *you* treat it that way. Other people will sort themselves out pretty quickly, or not. And wouldn't you rather know which of your relationships are built on something more than alcohol?

What I noticed, and what my friend noticed, was that each time I put my sobriety first, my self-esteem grew. It didn't always feel good in the moment — most times, the right choice was not the soft and squishy one — but the aftereffect was the balm my soul had been dying for. Over time, and with each right choice, I got stronger. I started to feel something magical growing inside me, getting bigger, more substantial, and pulsing with life.

Something like dignity.

In my first months sober, I did something radical for me. I showed up to work and *only did my job*. I didn't go above and beyond; I didn't crank out late nights and push myself to make people extra pleased and happy; I let some balls drop. And although it made me anxious at first, you know what I noticed?

Nothing happened. Like, nothing at all. Things kept going. Other people filled in the gaps. I started going to a noon 12-step meeting, and I stuck to it like…a doctor's appointment when I was pregnant. I didn't let other things fill that time — I just didn't let it happen. Even when the other stuff was "important" and I was "needed." I noticed that this same phenomenon applied to almost all areas of my life: my friendships, mothering, my family, my home.

After a while, I noticed that invitations started falling off. Some people stopped coming around. It was hard, but it was also okay. It's not that it didn't matter; it's that it *couldn't*. Not anymore.

Nothing Trumps the Process

Pregnancy lasts for nine months, give or take. It's never not been this way because someone wanted it to go faster, or slower (can you imagine?). We cannot change the process simply by having opinions about it or magical-thinking our way to sometime in the future when it's different, better, easier. A human life forms in the same miraculous way, no matter what we think about it. It doesn't matter how intelligent we are, how much experience we have, how much money we make, or how special we may think our circumstances are. We can do things to support or hurt the process, but we can't influence the process itself.

Pregnancy is both an act of choice and an act of allowing. An act of power and an act of surrender. Sobriety is not different.

As I said, the first half of my pregnancy was brutal. I thought it would never end. I didn't feel pregnant; I just felt sick. And subsequently resentful. I did everything to fight it and fix it, but nothing made the nausea move. Eventually, I learned to live with it, and right about the time that happened, it left.

Toward the end of my pregnancy, an ultrasound revealed that Alma was in a breech position. *Frank breech*, to be exact, which means that her butt (as opposed to her head, in a "normal" position) was facing the birth canal, and her knees were not bent with her feet pointing down but rather her legs were straight so that she was in a full pike position, with her feet up by her face.

This isn't a big deal; it's pretty common, and usually the baby turns on its own. Only 4 percent of babies are actually delivered breech.

I really wanted to have a natural birth, without drugs (this is funny, in hindsight), the old-fashioned way — through my hoo-ha — and, naively, I never considered it might not happen this way. But my doctor told us matter-of-factly that if the baby remained breech, she would have to do a C-section. It would be too risky otherwise. I pretended I wanted a natural birth because I was very worried about the potential damage of epidurals and such, but really, I just wanted to prove to myself and everyone else that I was really fucking tough and could handle a lot of pain. (I know.)

We tried everything to get her to turn. Acupuncture. Lighting incense at my feet. Yoga. Hypnosis. Talking to her. I even had a doctor perform a *version* — a painful procedure where they try to manually turn the baby. Nothing worked. Alma had no interest in moving.

In the end, having a C-section turned out to be just fine and didn't make me any less of a warrior or any less Alma's mother. I rarely think about how she was born.

Early sobriety wasn't all that different from pregnancy. I thought it should be...easier. Faster. Better. I never felt the elusive pink cloud people in recovery spoke of, just like I never felt the mysterious pregnancy glow. Most days were a confusing slog that I didn't understand. But once I stopped trying to fight it all so vehemently, once I let myself be at point A — which is where I actually *was* — things shifted. It didn't necessarily get easier. I just stopped suffering so much. As one of my friends said to me, "Laura, if you want to go faster, you have to slow down."

And like Kacey said, I could either flow with the stream of life or against it. But nothing was going to trump the process happening inside me.

You don't have to fight so hard, either.

I mean, you can, and you probably will. But you don't have to. Forming a new life is a really, really big deal. As John O'Donohue says in his blessing called "For the Interim Time,"

"It is difficult and slow to become new." It's supposed to be difficult. It's supposed to take everything you have. It's supposed to take longer than you want and to change you, completely. This often won't feel good when it's happening, but nothing worth having ever does.

Now I feel about sobriety much the same as I feel about becoming a mother: it has brought me right up to the nose of life itself and forced me to look it straight in the face. At first, the nearness was too much; there was nothing to protect me from the immediacy of things — not from the bright lights or the sharp pain. But then, eventually, I came to realize that this is what it really means to be alive — to not look away from any of it — and that all I was really doing before was pretending: floating through my days half-numb, half-involved, half-awake, thinking I was really *living* when in fact I was missing it all.

8

Fantasy Island

We are not mad. We are human.
We want to love, and someone must forgive us
for the paths we take to love,
for the paths are many and dark,
and we are ardent and cruel in our journey.

— LEONARD COHEN, "A Colony of Lepers"

I met Jon in AA. I'd noticed him around at a few meetings in Boston: his loud voice, his huge smile, the way he seemed to love being there when I did not. He was friends with many of the same people I'd met through my sponsor, Allison, and through her I learned he was a few years younger than I was and a lawyer, was "supersmart," and had been sober for almost a year.

We'd exchanged a couple of hellos at various parties but never really talked until a Fourth of July cookout in Boston. It was scorching hot that day, and I didn't want to be there but had nowhere else to be. When he walked up to me, I found my-self lighting up. He asked me about the words tattooed on my forearm: *beauty and terror*. I told him they were part of a Rilke poem, he said he knew who Rilke was, and then we were both impressed.

My love life then was a wasteland. This was the summer of 2014. Almost a full year had passed since my brother's wedding, and I'd yet to claim thirty consecutive days of sobriety. Many things had been tripping me up, but chief among them was how to connect or date or relate to men without drinking.

It had been two years since Jake and I separated. When I'd imagined my time after we split, I thought I would have all kinds of suitors, go on exciting dates, and maybe even find new love. I thought I would be stepping into some kind of powerful midthirties sexy streak, but I was running far too fast by then. I was sloppy, scared, and desperate.

With Jake gone, there was no one to watch me anymore. When he had been there, I hadn't wanted to be watched — I wanted to drink the way I wanted, to spend my time where and with whom I wished. But once he left, what little stability I had fell away.

We split the time with Alma evenly. When I had her, that was one thing. But when I didn't have her, I would rarely come home. I "dated" people, but not really. I busied myself with them. I disappeared into them. I slept with them. I made plans and drank too much. I blacked out. I scared people, or they scared me.

I created profiles on all the dating apps and dating sites — Tinder, OkCupid, Match — and met men over drinks. I met men while traveling for work. More than once, I went out with friends in Boston for brunch or lunch on the weekends and then just stayed out, by myself, drinking all day and night.

There was the bass player whom I met on Match who was newly "sober" but would "occasionally" go on benders; there was the old friend from high school who flew into town every now and then because his girlfriend lived near Boston; there was the 6'5" male nurse, and the gorgeous woman, and the kind Irish boy with blue eyes. I put myself into a dizzying stream of distraction and incapacitation and convinced myself I was doing something right, or was at least behaving normally for someone newly separated.

Thinking back to the morning after my brother's wedding, I can try to put the pieces of the puzzle together.

Once Alma had been accounted for, I somehow managed to pull myself together to make an appearance at the final brunch. After a surreal morning, Alma, my grandma, my mom, and I piled into our rental car to head back to my brother's house. Alma and I would spend the next couple of days there before heading back home to Boston.

I sat in the back with Alma, my stomach roiling both from the drinking and the dread, holding on to her little forearm as if it were my life raft. I had the window down, and a steady current of dry, hot July air hit my face. I knew, in a fractured way, that my life as I had known it was over, and I also kept thinking I could just step back in time. Press rewind. Stay in our hotel room. So easy.

It had only been one night. *A matter of hours.* It couldn't be real.

In *The Bright Hour,* a stunning memoir by Nina Riggs about her battle with terminal cancer, she describes the paradox of denial and also knowing that she would die when it became clear the end was close. She quotes a line from the French philosopher

Montaigne: "Did you think you would never reach the point toward which you were constantly heading?" This was it.

I was surprised.

I was not surprised.

I had known, maybe as far back as my first drink, that I would arrive there — but equally, I never imagined I really would.

On that ride home, I vaguely imagined what life might look like were I to stop drinking. Everything about it was inconceivable, but one thought especially sunk me.

How would I possibly find love?

Before I even got back to my car after the Fourth of July cookout — that first time we really talked — I sent Jon a friend request on Facebook. He accepted immediately, and we exchanged a few messages about how fun it was to run into each other. I suggested we hang out sometime, and he said he'd love that. The following Saturday, he rode the train up to my seaside town, and we set up chairs and a cooler of fizzy water at the beach down the street from my house.

We gushed about our favorite books: his, *Infinite Jest*; mine, *The History of Love*. We talked about AA, or "Secret Society," as he called it, and being sober. I'd learned from a mutual friend that about a month ago he had decided he wasn't ready to be sober — or rather, didn't really need to be — though he still occasionally went to meetings. We talked about that, and also where I was with things. I told him I had almost thirty days, but I didn't — it was something more like a week. I lied because I wanted him to think I was steadier than I was, as if a matter of days made a difference.

Since we'd made plans, my stomach had been flip-flopping in anticipation of seeing him. Now that we were on the beach and talking, I surprised myself with how overwhelmed I was by him, and also how drawn in I felt. At one point, he was talking about *Infinite Jest* and we were riffing on theories about David Foster Wallace and Mary Karr's romantic relationship when he started waving his arms around in big gestures of enthusiasm and his T-shirt sleeve lifted to reveal his upper arm — which had a touch of sunburn. It was also very muscular. I was overcome with a desire so strong, I had to look away.

We sat there for a couple of hours, and although we'd brought books, neither of us read a word. Despite his obvious interest in our conversation, I couldn't read him clearly: Did he like me? Was he interested? I couldn't tell, and this, coupled with my attraction to him and the surprising conversation — it was so rare to meet someone who wanted to talk about books and life in the same way I did — made me feel overcome by a growing cloud of melancholy.

"What's up? What're you looking at?" he asked.

My eyes were settled on a small island way off in the distance, just a few small bumps of land breaking the water's horizon.

A lump formed in my throat. I swallowed and kept my eyes fixed on the water. "It all feels that far away," I said, nodding toward the island.

"What does?"

"Everything. But especially love. It just feels impossible now."

"You mean because of sobriety?"

"Yeah."

I looked at him then, and he laughed his huge full-mouth

laugh. "Laura McKowen. You — more than almost anyone I can imagine — will have no problem finding love."

His words should have been a salve, but they weren't. They couldn't reach me. I was too new and too scared, and I didn't believe it. Plus, I wanted *him* to say he wanted me, not to speak in generalities about my desirability. It felt too much like the messages I'd heard all my life: "You're the marrying kind of girl, Laura, not the dating kind." Or "You're such a good friend; you're going to break a lot of hearts someday."

After we'd been there for a couple of hours, Jon looked at his watch and told me he needed to catch a train home shortly. We packed up, and as I was driving him back to the station, I kept having to push down the lump in my throat. I liked him, and without alcohol, there was nothing I could do to take the edge off the feelings or speed things up. I found myself entertaining all kinds of thoughts.

I had no idea how to do this sober. It wasn't the first instance when I'd spent time with a man without drinking, but it was definitely the first when it was not at least an option. In the past, if we were in different circumstances, I would have suggested we go grab food and drinks, and through the softening of alcohol, I would have flirted with him. There would have been easier conversation, teasing, more directness. We could charm each other. He would see how fun I am, how funny, and with his in- hibitions lowered in accordance with mine, he wouldn't be able to resist things moving forward. Instead of dropping him off at the train, I would have driven him home. He would have stayed.

But I knew — even with his recent departure from AA — that he and I would not be doing that particular dance. Drink- ing would not be a bridge to each other. And if drinking could not be a bridge to a man, was there another bridge? Even if Jon could have been interested in sober me, it didn't matter. I didn't know how to be her yet. I didn't even want to be her yet.

My ideas about love and what I had to do to get love are not unique. My guess is you've had them, too, or maybe still do. Somewhere along the line, you learned that you could not find love, or keep it, without shape-shifting yourself. Without altering certain aspects of your personality, forcing your body into an unnatural state, pretending to want things you do not want, or using drugs or alcohol to morph and medicate yourself. It is all the same thing. I am still uncovering the sneaky ways I try to earn love.

I used to roll my eyes at looking back on the past. Digging into my childhood for answers about my present patterns, blaming my parents or others for how I turned out — it seemed like a convenient rationalization, a bunch of psychobabble meant to excuse me from responsibility. But I've learned it's not at all about blaming. It's being willing to look at it all with clear eyes — to have compassion for the reasons people fell short but also to admit that they did. This was the hardest part: To admit that parts of my childhood were not okay. To stop protecting people. It is hard to type this even now, because I can hear voices telling me to stop playing the victim, that it wasn't all that bad. But I know that acknowledging the truth is actually an act of maturity and autonomy — it is, ironically, how we relieve ourselves from the victim role. Because once we are operating in reality, we can begin to take responsibility for what's ours, and stop taking responsibility for what never was. Denying works for only so long; eventually that shit will come out, and it will be ugly.

What was true for me is this:

My dad was, of course, the first man I loved. By all accounts, including his own, he is a very difficult man. I learned many wonderful things from him, but a steady love was not one of them. I learned to anticipate, predict, be hyperaware, and hustle in order to make things okay. I learned the ground can shift at any time, and when it does, it is my fault. I learned to lie, and I learned to deny. I learned that this was what love looked like, and that this was what it required.

All through my childhood and into high school, the entire boy thing — flirting, dating, having a boyfriend…all of it — was just so unreachable to me, like a place I could see or imagine but not actually visit. I became an athlete, I ran with the popular kids, I was pretty enough, but that only meant I was *supposed* to know how to do these things. While all my friends were holding hands at football games in high school, making out at parties, giggling about hand jobs and blow jobs and sex, talking on the phone late into the night, and going to homecoming and prom, I was standing by, embarrassed and confounded, wondering what the hell was wrong with me. It wasn't until alcohol came into the picture that I felt like I had a shot.

I discovered that the simple act of being willing to drink in high school put me in closer with the boys — *Look, I'm a fun girl!* Alcohol magically and swiftly rearranged me into whatever I hoped to be: a flirtatious, less self-conscious, outspoken, possibly even sexual version of Laura. And even though I was still too young to drink openly, I didn't think anything of doing it — it seemed like an eventuality, anyway. My family is a family of drinkers. Our culture is a culture of drinkers.

When I looked around me, I saw people drinking. I watched my parents interact with their friends, the people they dated, and later, their spouses, and alcohol was always just *there*, like milk in the fridge or soap in the shower. To me, it seemed like an inherent part of the adult picture of social interaction and intimacy.

Just before I went to college, my family closed down the Italian restaurant we owned to throw me a send-off party. I wore a tiny pair of white denim OP shorts and a tiny black Gap tank top, and I remember these things because the size of my body was my obsession. Midway through my senior year, it had become clear to me that my body was a problem. I was too athletic, too big, too *much*. So I starved it smaller.

I went on an extreme diet one of my girlfriends had mentioned and lost a bunch of weight fast. The weight loss was so satisfying that I did it again. Immediately, I got the attention I'd never had. Boys noticed. My friends noticed. My family — everyone. I was hooked. Before I knew it, I'd fallen down the rabbit hole of disordered eating: counting every calorie that crossed my lips (sugar-free gum = 10; toothpaste = 5) and restricting myself to a dangerously low number, exercising for hours a day, avoiding anything that might throw me off track.

By the time graduation came around, I didn't even look like myself. I'd lost far too much weight. I didn't want to keep shrinking but didn't know how to stop.

I had the typical late-adolescence stuff weighing on me then: I was unsure and excited about the future; I didn't really know who I was or who I'd become in college; I wanted desperately to be able to connect with boys. But there was other, heavier stuff, too.

My mom's marriage, her third then, was in trouble, and I knew it. Her husband, my stepfather, whom I adored, had inexplicably quit working and spent most of his afternoons and evenings shuffling around the restaurant bar talking to regulars, a glass of Dewar's on the rocks sweating in his hand, repeating himself in a half-gone stupor. My relationship with my biological dad was complicated and, at times, abusive, and though I would not come to really understand that or see that clearly for many years, it had etched deep grooves of pain inside me.

Because I was headed off to college, I was allowed to drink more or less freely at the restaurant by then. By late afternoon at my send-off party, I was on my third or fourth large tumbler of Bacardi and Diet Coke (few calories, high impact!).

As I headed back to the bar for a refill, I realized everything felt... *easy*. Smooth. The internal struggle was gone — like my cells had rearranged and organized me into a lighter, suppler presence. All the rigid calculations, the measuring, the tightness in my body melted. I couldn't even recall what I'd been so worried about. Everything in me vibrated in resonance to the music, the late-summer air, the people huddled around the bar. Previously frozen words poured out of my mouth as I gave warm hugs and kisses on cheeks. My body felt sexy instead of diminished. I could feel the shape of myself, strong and powerful and so perfectly small. Everything was possible.

I walked right behind the bar and scooped my tumbler into the ice as if I'd been practicing this move for years, filled it up, and then confidently added one, two, three, four fingers of rum. Our chef handed me the soda gun, and I sprayed the Diet Coke into the glass until it was full. We all clinked our glasses and said a cheers, and I swallowed a big swig — a whole mouthful of rum — my mouth and chest burning as it went down. "Holy SHIT!" I said, coughing, as my eyes watered, and we all laughed in camaraderie.

Everyone filed outside; I set the glass on the bar, grabbed a straw, and began stabbing at the ice to distribute the alcohol more evenly. I picked a slice of lemon from the container of garnishes and squeezed it in. I stood there, feeling my body in its sweet numbness. The world was perfectly smooth. Nothing hurt. I wasn't scared.

I thought, *If I can just stay like this, everything will be okay. If I can just stay like this... If I can just stay like this...*

When I think about those words now, they sound so simple and innocent, like something out of a Disney fairy tale. But they were a siren song. Like the passing sailors lured to their deaths by half-bird, half-woman creatures singing an irresistible melody, I truly believed alcohol would carry me and protect me. And I chased this idea for the next twenty years.

My senior year in college, practically decades after all my peers, I had sex for the first time. I was twenty-one. A friend — let's call him Mike — and I had run in the same circles since elementary school and got to be really close in high school. When he transferred to my college our sophomore year, we picked up the same dynamic from high school, just in a larger setting. I played the supercool friend, who watched his endless string of antics with girls while rolling my eyes, shaking my head, and occasionally comforting one who was particularly bereft by his behavior. All the while secretly wondering why I wasn't worth the attention.

The summer before our senior year, we both moved back home to work internships in Denver, and ended up spending a lot of time together at my family's restaurant in the evenings, huddled around the bar, drinking wine we couldn't afford and pretending to be grown-ups. Eventually, the drinking led to kissing, and the kissing led to more, but still no sex.

"*I* can't be your first," he would say, testing me, with his devilish grin, and I would mock-shove him away from me and agree, "No *way*."

Almost immediately when I'd gone off to college, the rubber band of starving myself snapped and I started to binge. By the end of my freshman year, I'd gained back all the weight that I had once lost, plus a bunch more. I felt totally out of control all the time, and I hated myself for it, every second of every day. Drinking was the only way I could put some space between me and the crushing shame.

I knew it only made me worse: drinking was a surefire way to ensure a massive binge, but at least when I was drunk, I cared less. Then morning would come, and I would swear myself off everything: drinking, eating, all of it. My journals from those days are brutal, repetitive, desperate. I couldn't stop the cycle. It was inconceivable to stop drinking in college. It was the only rite of passage I knew, the only way to connect with boys, and with my friends. I kept doing it because I didn't see a way *not* to and still exist.

I imagined that because this man friend of mine had known me for so long before I gained the weight, and because he really *knew* who I was and cared about me — or so I thought — he wouldn't see how my body had changed. Or at least he wouldn't mind.

When we returned to school in the fall, we stumbled to my house after the bars one night, and I'm not sure why it was time — there was no official conversation — but he took off my jeans, and basically that was that. I remember being grateful that I didn't have to take off my T-shirt and expose my stomach. It occurred to me to ask him to put on a condom, but I didn't want to slow things down or give him a reason to stop. Afterward, I told him I wasn't on the pill, and he said he'd figured as much, which was why he pulled out.

I didn't even know "pulling out" was a thing.

I was drunk. We both were. And every time we had sex after that was the same: we'd drink a lot, either together or separately, meeting up at the bar or at his house or mine, and he'd do his thing, and then we'd be done.

Drinking, paradoxically, both cheapened our connection to each other and brought us closer, though I saw only the latter at the time. That summer, we'd had all kinds of late-night, secret-divulging conversations fueled by the tongue-loosening effects of wine. We had fun, we got silly, we spent a bunch of time together, and ultimately, this led to getting physical. Alcohol helped me to distance myself from knowing he wouldn't look at my body, or in my eyes, when we were together, but it also allowed me to say things that were otherwise too hard for me to say sober: things I was too embarrassed to mention or ask about, like what we were doing together, what this thing was to him, how he felt about me.

I thought drinking made me bolder, more sexual, and sexier, and thus more desirable. I thought it brought out more of the *real* me, parts that just needed some help to emerge. Being buzzed gave me the warm, glowy sensation that there was something loving in our exchanges, even though they were only rushed and animalistic.

I got pregnant, no surprise.

The knowing hit me suddenly and absolutely, not because I remembered I missed my period (I had, by a lot) or because my boobs were tender (they were, very) but in the way women know things before they're proved. I weaved through the smoke and the crowd at the bar and whispered it into his ear. He assumed it was a false alarm, but a few minutes later, back at my apartment, two blue lines confirmed I was right.

Even then, I tried to make the situation okay for him. I worried that if I freaked out, he would leave, so I played it cool. I knew neither one of us wanted to have a baby, but I hoped the situation would endear me to him and bring us closer. That by talking about it, and dealing with it together, we would bond, and I would mean something different to him. But there was nothing after that night. A week later, a friend drove me to the clinic and waited. I paid for it all myself on a credit card. He never said anything about it again.

Four months later, just before graduation, I drove to his house early one Saturday morning. In a rare moment of clarity and anger, I planned to tell him how terrible he was for treating me the way he had and how I didn't deserve it. When I pulled up, he was walking out the front door of the house he shared with our mutual friends. As we faced each other in the driveway, I surprised us both by screaming at the top of my lungs; I have no idea what I said, only that when his mouth started to curl into a smirk, I quickly lost my steam.

When I finished, he said, "You've got red splotches on your chest, Laura. Are you upset?" He nodded at me, the way cocky boys nod at objects. He was trying not to laugh.

I stared at him for a moment, searching in vain for some sign of compassion on his face, and then got into my silver Honda Civic, backed out of the driveway, and drove home.

I convinced my friend Jen to go to our favorite bar together, and we sat at a high table and drank Stoli Razberi and Sprite until I couldn't feel anything anymore. We agreed that he was a horrible human — an awful, disgusting, shit person who never deserved another breath from me. The vodka and our conversation stirred up the anger inside me, but once it wore off, I sank back into the swallowing hole of rejection.

What haunts me still is that even after all that, I still hoped he would come around. I waited for him to call. I looked for him when I was running around campus or out with my friends. I wanted him to choose me. I wanted him to love me. I wanted him to tell me I was worth something.

This pattern continued throughout my twenties as my relationships with men and drinking became braided even more tightly together. The alcohol was a way to connect, the bridge to intimacy — not *only* in romantic relationships, but especially in them. I believed it was the way in, a sort of magic trickery. I believed love happened only on some other island — a metaphorical place in my mind where all the right people lived.

On the island, everyone was attractive and intelligent, and their bodies were whipped into shape. They married their soul mates, started families, got advanced degrees and big promotions, and they drank endlessly and effortlessly with no real consequences. My friends all lived on the island; so did the people I worked with. Anyone worth knowing lived there. It was a place I built based on the false narrative that this was what it meant to really be alive. In my narrative, you had to live on the island to live the good life. It was what I saw growing up; it's what is marketed to us; it's the common belief in a culture of *more, faster, now, better*.

Even as my drinking clearly became destructive, I didn't see it as the problem. I saw *myself* as the problem. This was how it worked on the island; the drinking was a marker of a good life, of doing it right. Everyone else on the island seemed to be doing fine with it all, so clearly I just needed to try harder.

When I was faced with sobriety, I only saw evidence that my love life would be cut off at the knees were I to stop drinking. Even my relationship with Jake had started while we were drinking, and much of our courtship included it. Not excessively, and not exclusively, but it was a consistent thread throughout.

We met at that party on Cape Cod — a weekend-long drink-and-drug-fest party. One of our first dates was a NASCAR race in the Poconos, and having found ourselves quite outside our natural habitat, we began exploring the grounds for something to do. After a while, we hit a jackpot: an apple-martini bar set up on a card table! We played horseshoes, we drank too many of those sweet things, and on the walk back to find our friends, he told me he was falling for me.

Months later, at a summer lobster party in Maine, I confessed for the first time that I loved him, late at night in our tent, my head buzzing with vodka and new love. That fall, after he'd gone off to law school, he came back for Halloween weekend, and we got dressed up: he in a huge wig and a minister's robe, I as Jackie O. We went to a bar party with all our friends, and later in the night, with OutKast blasting and a few beers in, he leaned in close so my face was smooshed into that enormous wig and said the words I'd been waiting to hear: "I'm in love with you, too."

Wine on date nights. Cocktails with friends. Long, lazy Sunday brunches. Our engagement, wedding, holidays, birthdays, vacations. Drinking had punctuated all those moments.

I wondered whether we would have even met had I not been

drinking. One night in the first months of trying at sobriety, lying in bed after Alma had gone to sleep, in a rare unguarded moment on the phone with him, I asked. He considered it for a moment.

"I don't know, Laura. Maybe not. We met at a party. But who you were drinking is not why I loved you."

This is the irony of it all. I was confused about that then, and I often still am. Real love — as I have known it — has always been willing to meet me where I am.

Jake. Alma. Some of my friends and family. They only ever wanted me to be who I was.

But I couldn't see it that way because I couldn't stand to be there — in my center. I didn't know how to. I never had. And so *they* became the problem; I perceived them to stand between me and what I needed. Getting sober meant I had to choose to leave the island for good, which felt like leaving behind every chance I would ever have at love. I happened to be single when I was facing sobriety, but I've learned this is a question asked by nearly everyone who broaches sobriety, regardless of their relationship status.

Many of my married friends have wondered if their relationship would survive if they quit, even in the cases where alcohol has caused significant and obvious damage. Others have been told by their partners that they don't have a problem and just need to chill out, cut back, "stop being so dramatic"; and the subtext they hear is: *Don't change. I won't like it (and I might not even like you) if you do.*

One of my best friend's longtime relationship ended when she got sober because her boyfriend said he couldn't relate to her any longer. She was too uptight, he said. Not as much fun. He didn't "know how to be with" her anymore. This is not all that uncommon — all relationships go through a period of recalibration after major change, and some find their way to a new, stronger baseline, while others don't. When you're on the receiving end of such news, it cuts about as deep as anything (and, unfortunately, keeps a lot of people in the cycle of destructive behaviors). But the reality is, any relationship built on a foundation of partial inebriation is a lie, anyway. What my friend's boyfriend was really saying to her was this: *I like a version of you that is less...you. And I like a version of us that is at least a slight departure from reality.*

I truly thought drinking made me *more of* who I was. I thought it made life more possible, not less, by opening up opportunities to connect and brightening my personality. I thought it brought out the true in me and the true in others, so that we could really see each other and bond. This didn't just go for romantic relationships; it was the same at work, with my friends, with family.

Leaving it behind felt like exile in so many ways, because *it was*. I would never take a trip to the island again. At least, theoretically. All the people who lived on the island would see me only when we decided to meet elsewhere.

As for people who lived in this new land of sobriety, I wondered if love and happiness and beauty and sex appeal were really possible for them.

I wanted to believe they were. But in order to do that, I would have to relearn everything.

I don't have a neatly wrapped-up lesson to offer you here. Not yet. But perhaps you can see a little more clearly the ways in which you've left the center of yourself in order to get to love. Even more importantly, you might see how you didn't do whatever you did to get love because you are weak, or broken, or wrong. You sought love simply and only for the same reasons I did, and still do: because this is how we are wired. As *A Course in Miracles* states, all human behavior is either love or a call for love. *All human behavior.* Once I started to look at it this way, it softened my shame about my patterns with men and also why I sought so much solace in drinking. It allowed me to see myself as someone who was hurting, instead of someone who was weak.

What I am coming to see, very slowly and over time, is that nothing that requires or causes me to abandon myself is really love. Love is a mirror that reflects you back to yourself, not a portal through which you jump into oblivion. It doesn't ask you to be different. It doesn't secretly wish you were. Yes, a relationship is always going to be a compromise, but when you start compromising *yourself,* it becomes something else. A hostage situation, maybe. An arrangement. A use. An abuse. I have been on both sides of all these scenarios.

Jon and I continued to date off and on in my first two years of sobriety. Eventually we parted ways because he had to get sober himself, and he did. He had buoyed me to sobriety by holding up the vision of who I was becoming — before I could see her. He once told me, "I feel like right now you are the raw stuff of creation: mud, and manna, and pure power. And I get to watch you in the first part of becoming. You have no idea how much potential is inside of you." And he says I helped him get sober later, by power of example. We often joke that we survived each other, and it's true, but we also survived because of each other.

A couple of times in recent years we've questioned whether our relationship would work now that we are both sober, but ultimately, it's just not like that. We were excellent catalysts for each other but terrible partners.

Since then, I've dated over the years, once or twice at length. Over time it's become more intentional and grounded, less caustic and juvenile. I can hold my center a little longer, or at least identify when I've left it and return more quickly. I don't obsess over dead-end men and relationships, and I don't project all my needs and pain onto every man I come across like I did in the beginning. I haven't found *the* Love but also don't believe in the panacea of that anymore.

In all of it, I've learned a few things — about love, about the island, about myself.

One thing is that I was never going to find real love on the island, because being there meant I had left myself. So it wasn't *me* showing up; it was someone else. You will never find it there, either, on the island, whatever that island looks like for you — that imaginary place you have to go to in order to feel wanted or sexy or desirable or normal. The place where we pretend, in big ways and in small, that we are something or someone we know in our bones we are not. We can go a long time pretending and thinking we're doing it right this way, building big, complicated lives on a false foundation. No matter how big and impressive a life you build there, on that island, the crumbling of that life is inevitable.

Who I need to be to get love is still the question — likely, the work of my life. But sobriety has allowed me to inch closer, layer by layer, to her, to the center of myself. By learning to stay in the moments when I had always run before, I have learned her contours and her design. I have started to know her. And to trust her.

I can feel her when I look at the ocean. When I smell Alma's head. When I write these words to you.

I feel her, and then I run.

I feel her, and then I leave her again.

But I come back. Each new day that I am here without dimming myself by drinking, I have a chance to come back and try again. And I do.

9

A Bigger Yes

Sometimes I can hear my bones straining
under the weight of all of the lives I'm not living.

— JONATHAN SAFRAN FOER,
Extremely Loud and Incredibly Close

I didn't want to go.

Months before my mom's sixtieth birthday party — before I met Jon, before I started wrestling with what it meant to be in love and be sober — I committed to go on a four-day yoga retreat with two of my friends at Kripalu, a world-renowned wellness center in western Massachusetts. When we booked it, I'd been excited, assuming I'd be well into my sobriety by then and feeling solid and secure. I also figured it would help strengthen my resolve to stay sober — a futile tactic I'd been using for years to try to backdoor my way into repair.

If I refuse to buy clothes in a bigger size, I'll be motivated to lose the weight.

If I sign myself up for another marathon, it'll keep me out of trouble on the weekends.

If I keep buying books about weight loss, it'll happen by osmosis.

If I make more money, I'll start paying off my debt.

If I sign up for a writing course, or another writers' retreat, or make more friends who are writers, I'll definitely start writing.

If I commit to this diet, I'll drink less.

When it came time to go in October 2014, I had barely strung together twenty days of sobriety since my mom's birthday. I was jittery and on edge and kicking myself for signing up. The whole thing, a yoga weekend in the majestic Berkshire Mountains, seemed frivolous and fraudulent.

For one, I was broke. Despite the fact that I made good money, I was still living paycheck to paycheck every month. There was a mountain of unopened mail on my kitchen counter — IRS bills, parking tickets, credit-card statements — and the week before I'd been pulled over for having expired license plates and an expired inspection sticker. The police officer then unfortunately discovered I *also* had a very expired license and told me with a glare of contempt that if it wasn't for Alma being in the car with me, he'd arrest me.

Instead, we piled into the seamless gray plastic back seat of his police cruiser — Alma and me — and the officer asked me endless questions as I tried not to cry. I thought: This *is the reality of my life.* This *moment is telling me the truth about where I am.*

Going away for the weekend to do yoga felt ridiculous.

Also, things had started to pick up with Jon and me. It was immature and shortsighted of me, but I didn't want to be disconnected from him right now. I didn't want to miss the possibility of seeing him on a kid-free weekend.

Above all, I was exhausted. I loved my friends, but being in a car for hours and sharing a room and having to talk and participate in the world without the comfort of my bed and little routines sounded awful and like way too much. These two friends both knew I was working at sobriety, but they didn't know — still, no one really knew — exactly where I stood.

Part of this was that I just couldn't speak about it all yet. I was too ashamed and scared, and the longer it went on, the harder it got to come clean. But part of my withholding was about me wanting to keep a fire door open. I still wanted an out to keep drinking, even if it was subconscious. As long as people thought I was generally doing okay, they would leave me be and not watch too closely.

My first yoga class was at Baptiste Power Yoga in Cambridge in 2002. Baptiste yoga is an intense, athletic style of vinyasa yoga done in a hot room, usually above eighty-five degrees. There was a studio down the street from my apartment, and one random Wednesday after work, a group of us went from the office together.

Everything about this yoga class was different from any other type of exercise I'd done: the heated room that smelled of incense and sweat, the quiet (no music was played in classes then), the focus on breath, the rigor of each pose. Although I had been an athlete all my life and a consistent runner, these classes were grueling for me. Within twenty minutes, I would find myself shaking, out of breath, looking for the door, a way out.

I kept going on occasion, maybe once or twice a month, for years, because I loved the physicality of it. It didn't hurt my body the way running did, yet it felt just as intense, if not more.

I was also attracted to something I could not name at the time. While 99 percent of the class would be an extraordinary grind, there would be an occasional moment, maybe only a breath or two, when my eyes would be within an inch of my shin bone or the curve of my shoulder — so close that I could see individual pores and freckles on my skin. Every muscle in my body would be twitching, sweat would be stinging my eyes, and I could feel my heartbeat in my ears. In those moments, my attention narrowed to a single point of focus.

The intensity of the practice had absorbed me. My mind — which was always racing, fast and loud — slowed. The world went quiet. I could feel new layers of myself emerging. I was learning to be present, though I didn't have a name for it then.

In 2008, I signed up for my first yoga teacher training. I decided to do it on a whim after I'd taken a class at a new studio in my neighborhood in South Boston. It was such a different style than Baptiste that I could barely even believe it was considered yoga. As I left the studio, I saw a flyer on the door advertising their teacher training starting the following week. I got what I now call a "hit" in my belly — that intuitive nudge, or a knowing feeling in the body — that I needed to do it. When I got home, I went on their website and immediately signed up. I didn't even talk to Jake about it first.

The next day, I found out I was pregnant. I wrongly assumed I would have to defer my spot, and as the morning sickness took over in the weeks that followed, I almost begged off dozens of times, but the studio owner, David, urged me to stay with it.

The training turned out to be a saving grace in those lonely months of my pregnancy, when I was feeling so sick and unsure. I learned about The Work of Byron Katie and the works of Patanjali. I dabbled in the yoga sutras and anatomy. I was pushed far, far outside my comfort zone by doing things like staring into someone's eyes for twenty minutes consecutively and confronting emotional discomfort in myself and others without the mollification of alcohol. I had no formal plan to teach, but I knew being there was going to change things for me nonetheless.

Throughout the training, I thought over and over again about how narrowly I had almost missed the opportunity — how if any number of things had gone differently, I wouldn't have been there. If my friend hadn't canceled on me the morning before that first class at David's studio and caused me to change my plans, if I had gone to my usual Baptiste studio instead of trying a new place, if I had taken a class with another instructor whom I didn't like as much, or if I'd waited to talk to Jake before signing up and found out I was pregnant first, I wouldn't have been there.

Things like this were always happening in my life. People, situations, and opportunities were always showing up to help me out or lead me to the next step. But when I was drinking, I was too distracted or unconscious to see them, let alone follow the bread-crumb trail they were leaving for me. In sobriety, I started to see very quickly just how supported I had been all along.

This is something I rely on implicitly now. This isn't the part of the book where I tell you that you have to take a leap of faith or believe God is Good or buy into some planetary-alignment psychic woo-woo magical thinking. What I'm saying is that things are actually happening *for* you all the time — that there's a much larger thing going on here than your own singular existence — and that it's possible you can trust where it's leading you. I don't know what you'll have to give up to see it. For me it was drinking. For you it might be something different. What I'm saying is, it will be worth it to hear the sound of that small voice inside you again.

After Alma was born, I began teaching my first yoga class. Monday nights in a dark, dingy room at the YMCA in Salem, Massachusetts. I taught that class for two years, and even though I often had to drag myself there after a full day of working in Boston, teaching filled me up. It also *terrified* me. I didn't sleep the night before I taught my first class. My hands and my voice shook every single time I began a class for the first year, and red splotches broke out across my chest, so I'd often wear a sweatshirt to cover it, even when the room was a sauna. I taught classes for one person and classes for forty. Every time, I loved it. The littlest things brought me joy: creating the playlists, finding a new way to cue a pose, reading bits of poetry at the end of class. All of this felt like sweet, fresh air. It was in such contrast to the rest of my life, especially my work life.

Still, I never aspired to jump into it full-time.

By that fall when the Kripalu retreat came around, I wasn't teaching yoga anymore, and I was barely even practicing. Being with myself like that was too hard emotionally. So when I walked into that retreat that weekend — a room packed with over one hundred people lined up on mats, strong and confident, and a woman named Seane standing at the front of the room, ready for our attention — I felt panicked. Before she even said anything, I could feel my heart hammering out of my chest.

Over the weekend, she talked about trauma in the body, the responsibility of healing so we have something to offer ourselves and each other; about using yoga not just as a way to feel or look better but as a way to change the world; and about the importance of using our lives — how each individual life mattered so much. It was nothing I hadn't heard before, but the way she said it, and the conviction she had, stoked something inside me.

From her very first words, I kept hearing something primal in me scream, *I want to do this! I want to do this! I want to do this!*

But, do *what*? Teach yoga to hundreds of people? Become an activist? Grow my hair long and impossibly, luxuriously curly?

Every time the thought *I want to do this* arrived, my mind would counter, *Who do you think you are?* But something else was also happening in the background, a layer deeper. A seed of unshakable knowing was taking root. As absurd as it was — as distant as the reality of my life was from what she was doing — I also knew it was already written inside me. I knew I would do it. I knew I *could*, if I stayed sober.

I find that often, just when we begin to become resolute about things in our lives, something happens to unsteady us. I think it's life's way of saying, *You sure? Show me.* So it's no big surprise to me that Jon went dark on me that weekend.

Things had been going well with us at that time; we'd been spending consistent time together and falling for each other more. But right when we pulled into the parking lot at Kripalu, he texted me and told me to "have a great weekend" in a way that indicated he would be signing off. I should have welcomed the reprieve so I could focus on what I was doing, but I was countries away from being that grounded at the time. This had been our pattern: We'd be going along somewhat steadily, and then out of nowhere, he'd break things off or disappear. Usually, it was to drink, which was, of course, the ultimate mindfuck. A few weeks later, we'd regroup and swear to be more consistent, and then without fail, it would happen again. Each time was worse than the last, because at that point I knew I was doing it to myself.

More than once over the weekend, I left the room under the guise of "going to the bathroom" just so I could check my phone for his texts. *Silence.* I lay in bed at night replaying our text conversations in my head, or thinking of ways to punish him for not speaking to me. Three days felt like three weeks without an air supply. If I had been closer to home or by myself at the retreat, I probably would have left. But I was stuck.

I also ached desperately for Alma. I had tried to call Jake to catch her a few times, but we kept missing each other.

As the hours passed, and then the days, the storms of emotion rolled through me — from confusion, to sadness, to self-righteous anger, to rage, to emptiness…and then all of it all over again. I was forced, for the first time, to stay. When I wanted to keep checking my phone, I couldn't; when I wanted to run out of the room, I couldn't. At least not without disrupting everything. When I wanted to keep turning over the conversations with Jon in my mind, I was forced out of it by the physical difficulty of a pose. I wanted to listen to Seane only a teeny-tiny fraction more than I wanted to bail, so I stayed, and I stayed, and I stayed.

It felt like my skin was burning off.

On Sunday morning, the closing of the retreat, Seane mentioned we could come talk with her afterward if we liked. I've never been the kind of person to do that kind of thing, but

I knew I couldn't stay comfortable anymore. I wanted to tell her what I had not been able to tell anyone else yet: that I was twenty-two days sober, that doing this was the hardest thing I had ever done, that I was scared — so scared. I told myself to do what Kacey had told me to do when I was afraid to go to my first meeting, which was to just get my body there.

Our bodies are always our bridge back home.

When Seane finished speaking, I jumped up from my mat and did that — I forced my body to the front of the room. As I approached, I could feel those hot red splotches splattering across my neck and chest, and my legs went numb. I was the first one to reach her.

"I am twenty-two days sober today," I blurted out, and she grabbed my hands and nodded. "This is the hardest thing I have ever done," I gasped. She hugged me.

She told me that she had all the respect in the world for me, that it was a tough-ass ride, but that she knew lots of people who'd done it and she knew I could, too. We chatted a little more, and she gave me a few tips.

"You can totally do it," she said when we parted.

God, how I wanted to believe that.

As we were getting ready to leave the retreat that weekend, I took another spin through the bookstore. On one of the racks, I saw a book called *The Great Work of Your Life*, by Stephen Cope. I picked it up and started thumbing through it, and a quote from the Gospel of Thomas caught my eye: "If you bring forth what is within you, what you bring forth will save you; if you do not bring forth what is within you, what you do not bring forth will destroy you."

Reading those words, I felt my whole body turn to goose-flesh.

If you do not bring forth what is within you, what you do not bring forth will destroy you.

That was it.

That's what had been screaming at me all weekend.

I knew two things:

One: that if I did not allow whatever was in me to come forth — being a teacher, a leader, a (dare I say it?) writer — I would lose my life. This unused potential inside me was not imagined, nor was it benign. If I didn't use it, it would not just sit there, dormant. Something dark and destructive would grow in its place. It already had.

Kacey had said to me a while back that addiction is the pain of being disconnected from God. This felt true to me, even though I had never worshipped a God in the traditional sense. It felt true in that when I drank, I felt severed from the basic good-ness in myself, from a larger current of possibility and ineffable beauty and truth. To me, this was the most painful reality of drinking: the deadness, the flattening of my spirit — although I had never articulated it that way.

Two: I knew in that moment that what I'd felt rising up in me as I listened to Seane that weekend, what I'd felt emanating from her and transmitting through me when I heard *I want to do this* ringing in my head over and over, was the truth of what wanted to come forth trying to reach me.

For so long, all I could see was what I would be losing by giving up drinking — love being only one representation of many. Despite all the aphorisms and positive thinking and stories I'd heard from other sober people promising me otherwise, all I could feel was the loss. Augusten Burroughs, in his book *This Is How*, said that what worked for him in getting sober was to find something he loved more than drinking. I understood that intellectually, and it sounded awfully catchy and inspiring, but it just didn't feel true for me.

Being in that room with Seane, feeling whatever had been sparking up in me — even in the midst of all the emotional angst and discomfort — I started to get it. For the first time, I could imagine chasing something bigger.

Here's what is true, for you and for me: the grief and the sadness are real. When you give up something you've relied on as heavily as I relied on alcohol, even when that something is actively destroying your life, it is a true loss. You can't deny that, and more importantly, you don't have to.

I thought there was something wrong with me for feeling so heartbroken. How could I actively miss a thing that had nearly cost me everything, including Alma?

There was nothing wrong with me, though. *Alcohol had been my friend.* It had carried me through a lot of pain I might have otherwise not been able to withstand. It had softened experiences that needed to be softened. It had been there for me always, without question. My drinking — and whatever it is you do to feel better — was born of a natural impulse to soothe, to connect, to feel love. And although alcohol hadn't actually delivered those things, it was absolutely yoked to them in my mind. In my heart and body, too. It was just what I knew.

So of *course* I was terrified without it. Of *course* I missed it. The absence of it was terrible. And necessary. Maybe it's helpful to linger there for a minute, in the terrible and the necessary. To start to see them as the same. Maybe in this way, pain is not such a problem.

When I saw Seane up there, doing what she did, I realized it wasn't in spite of her pain that she was doing these things but because of it. She knew exactly what it took to walk through the fire. That is what I recognized in her. That was why I believed her.

Because that strength was in me, too.

I had always quashed my pain and cut it off before it could burn all the way through. I drank it away or ate it away or disappeared into another person or work. Being there over those four days, without contact with Jon or Alma or the comforts of home, had given me a taste of what it was like to just let it burn. I felt it. I felt it all over my body. And although it was excruciating most of the time, there were a few moments when I surrendered the fight and simply allowed everything to wash over me. In those moments, I found that right alongside the sharp intensity and unease, there was some small part of me willing to stay, another voice softly saying, *I am willing to be here.*

Behind all those *no*s and *never-again*s is a much bigger *yes*. It might not seem clear now, but it will be clear soon. Listen to the voice. Listen to your body. This is in you already.

There is a life that is calling you forward, begging you to meet its eye, to glimpse its vision for you. You can get only so far by running away from what you do not want. Eventually you will have to turn toward what you do. You will have to run toward a bigger yes.

10

The Truth about Lying

The truth is the thing I invented so I could live.
— NICOLE KRAUSS, *The History of Love*

I never considered myself a liar.

In fact, I prided myself on being a fierce confronter of the truth, especially if it wasn't pretty. I was always willing to "go there" with people: to look at the harder parts of life, talk about your crippling depression or your family's bankruptcy or your sister's addiction to painkillers. Small talk bored me. I wanted to get to the heart of things and look at what was *really* going on.

As a kid, I'd perch up on the stairs in my mom's house, out of view, listening intently to her talk with her friends, hoping to be let in on the inner life of adults — the parts they tried to hide when kids were around. I gravitated toward dark music, books, and movies. Give me some Cat Power and some Sylvia Plath and some *Leaving Las Vegas* and I was set for a party.

To keep me away from manning the music when we got together, my friends joked, "We're good with the depression rock
for a while, Laura." I have always been able to sit with people in
pain, to look straight into the darker corners of our emotional
landscapes without flinching. I thought this meant I had a real
relationship with the truth.

But somehow — as I rounded the corner into my thirties —
I found myself swimming in lies. Lying. All the time.

I hadn't noticed it happening; there was no decision or
abrupt change in direction: *Now, I am going to lie.* It was a grad-
ual turning away and shrinking: a small twist of words here,
a detail left out there, a matter of fractions of millimeters at a
time, and suddenly I found myself boxed into a very small room.

Jake and I had been married for a short time, maybe a year.
We sat down to eat dinner one night at our hand-me-down
kitchen table, enclosed in the soft mint-green-colored walls of
our kitchen — a color I chose just before we moved in. I have no
idea what we ate that night, what day of the week it was, or what
season we were in, but I remember looking at him and watching
his mouth move as he spoke. This was a boy (he was a boy then;
we were just kids) whom I'd loved so innocently and completely
from the start, yet I was deceiving him.

I don't mean I was nursing a few private thoughts about
my job that I hadn't let him in on yet, or that I secretly disliked
one of his friends. I'd been actively lying — by omission, if not
directly at times — in ways I never thought I was capable of.
Worst of all, I hadn't noticed the totality of the distance I'd created between us until it was so big that I could physically feel it.

I'd started to have thoughts about other men. I drank behind his back sometimes, refilling my glass secretly in the kitchen or taking swigs from bottles of beer or vodka — like a kid sneaking a cookie when they could just as easily ask for one. I had done cocaine at parties we were at together, and he had no clue. Most painfully and surprisingly, I sometimes — often, too often, for reasons I could not yet justify or explain — wished I'd never married him. I wished I could press rewind and take it all back.

He was still unsuspecting of me then, and why wouldn't he be? I'd been unsuspecting, too. I'd been true-blue for him without trying from the moment we met, and then something within me began to shift. I started to turn away from him, and though I hated myself for it, I didn't know how to stop.

I looked for reasons we weren't right so I could justify my turning, but they were hard to find, so I looked for reasons *he* wasn't right.

At that point, we were still new, with so much momentum. We had an entire promising future spread out before us. It wasn't until later that he would start to confront me: about the drinking, about whether I was interested in other people, about my seemingly growing contempt for him.

It was the innocence in his face that evening, this presumption of commitment and integrity on my part, that gave me pause. I mean, why would he assume otherwise, when all I had done was adore him? I had fallen into lockstep with him immediately, both of us so sure of where we were headed and how we felt. Sitting there, with just a few physical feet between us, I thought, *I have an entire world inside me that you know nothing about.*

With just a few words, I could change that. I could create one reality again, instead of two. But I didn't. I couldn't.

How fragile this was. How powerful. They were just words:

sounds I could make with my mouth. But if I never made them, he would never know. And strangely I believed *I* wouldn't have to know, either. I believed if I could only hang on for long enough, eventually it would all disappear inside me, like salt dissolving into water.

Technically, of course, I made a choice that night. I'd been making choices all along, even if I didn't always realize it. But I truly did not consider there to be any choice in that moment. I would never tell him what was really going on with me. The price was too high. Many times I thought, *I'd rather die.*

This is the dilemma of dishonesty. In order to keep one lie going, you have to tell more lies. Eventually, you will paint yourself into a place where winning is impossible. Even if the lies are never found out, you begin to rot from the inside out. The deception contaminates you. And then it contaminates your relationship.

At first, I was just hiding my ambivalence. Then I was hiding what I was doing to try to not feel my ambivalence: drinking more, testing flirtations, sowing seeds of contempt. While drinking, I acted out, and while sober, I drank to kill the shame of that. All the while, I lied more and more. I lied about things big and small, serious and inane: whom I was going to happy hour with, whether or not I'd replied to an email from Alma's preschool, what I felt and wanted. Eventually, it became habitual, second nature, as reflexive as sneezing. Similar to drinking, I was blind to the reality of what was happening, and what I could see, I justified.

I told myself I was protecting him, us, our little family. I was staving off unnecessary conflict. I was trying to be kind.

This was all, of course, bullshit. I didn't have the courage to be honest, or the perspective or tools to know how to, so I made everything chaotic and then blamed him. He wasn't *fun* enough. We were too *different*. He was *judgmental*. He didn't *get* me. I was *lonely*.

The truth was, I was terrified. I didn't want to lose him or shatter his opinion of me. I was also getting swallowed whole by addiction, and neither of us really knew it.

Being in a relationship with someone who is addicted is a lot like living with infidelity. It's no different from your partner having a lover, except the lover isn't another person but a thing. Having been on both sides of the equation — the addicted, and the one watching someone I love in the throes of it — I can say this is hauntingly accurate. If there's one thing you can count on, it's that addiction will always demand *more*: more attention, more loyalty, more time. More everything.

I imagined that when Jake and I separated, I would be released from the burden of lying. I thought my insides would simply straighten out, back to the way I was — or at least the way I had perceived myself to be — before things had gone so wrong. I thought he was, or at least *we* were, the central issue, and that if we were done, I would eventually settle back into the shape of something better and more whole. Ideally, we both would.

Several months after we separated, my friend Jason invited me to his house one Saturday morning. We worked together and had become good friends. He'd gone through a divorce a couple of years earlier, and I'd confided in him when it was clear things were heading in that direction for Jake and me. As is typical in advertising, we worked hard and played harder, driving toward endless deadlines and supplementing our efforts with a lot of drinking and entertaining for clients. This had made us all pretty close.

I was nervous to head over to his house. A Saturday-morning invite for coffee wasn't totally odd but odd enough that it felt ominous. I expected I'd done something I didn't remember or was otherwise in trouble. We'd all been going out a lot lately, and I more so since I now had child-free nights when Alma was with Jake. I felt some relief when I arrived and there was nothing but warmth on his face, but still there was a knot in the pit in my stomach.

He hugged me, sat me down at his kitchen table, and gave me toast with honey and Teddie Super Chunky peanut butter and coffee. He slid a bowl of chocolate-covered almonds between us, because that was our favorite snack, and then paused. I squeezed my sweaty hands together under the table.

He said, "First, I didn't bring you here to yell at you or scold you or fight. But I wanted to tell you something, because I care about you and I see something that I think you don't."

"Okay." Cue the hives.

"You don't have to lie."

What?

"I know —" I interrupted. My favorite sentence, *I know.*

"No — I mean it. I see you do it all the time, even when you don't have to."

I started to get defensive but then stopped myself. I asked him for examples, and he gave me a few. "You lied to Jake on the phone the other day about something dumb. I heard you. You lied about why you were late for work when you didn't have to. You lied about losing your computer." I started crying.

"You're beautiful and wonderful, and you don't have to lie. I don't know why you do it, but I want you to know you don't need to — especially not with me, okay?"

I nodded, unable to say anything yet. I was ashamed — just so steeped in shame all the time then. It never left me, and it was like he had pulled back a curtain and there I was, naked. And it wasn't that I felt judged by him; it was that I didn't. It was the kindness that broke me.

I sat there crying for a while — as long as I could tolerate. We talked a little longer about lighter things: work gossip, renovations he was planning on his new place, music. When I got up to leave, he grabbed my shoulders and squared me toward him.

"One more thing," he said.

Oh Jesus, what? I laughed nervously.

"The drinking. It seems to have a deleterious effect on you." He enunciated each syllable in "deleterious" so that it came out slowly: *del-e-te-ri-ous.*

I nodded a quick "okay" and started to grab my coat. We were not going there.

"Hold on." He made me look at him again before he continued. "You don't need it." He waited for me to acknowledge that I'd heard him. "Okay?"

"Okay." I nodded.

"All right, get out of here."

When I think about the theories I had for so long about love and drinking, here is a story that doesn't fit. Here is one of those moments that has helped me change my mind about this. Because if you can't have love without drinking, then how was it possible that right here, in the middle of my biggest mess, I had it?

There are a thousand other stories I could tell of people who loved me, people who saw the real me even when I was doing everything I could to show them otherwise. I could write another whole book of these stories. Jason is just one of them.

But the reason I bring it up at all is to show you how common it is — how totally Saturday morning and casual it is — for us to be loved without even knowing it.

I'm sure you know what it's like to hear something that you can't unhear — when a little piece of truth lodges itself into your psyche and won't leave you be, no matter how hard you try to erase it. While not much outwardly changed because of what Jason had said — my drinking went on just as it had before, and continued to worsen quickly — I started to notice how often I reflexively lied, even about silly things, like whether or not I'd seen a movie or liked a certain song.

If I thought that a lie would improve your opinion of me or create a connection between us, chances are that I would say it without even noticing until after the words had left my mouth. I also started to notice how paranoid I'd become, how *prepared* I was to lie at any given moment. When I saw Jake's name come up on my phone, got a text from a friend, or went to check my Facebook messages, dread would automatically fill my throat, even when there wasn't an obvious problem. *What does he know? What am I going to have to explain? What is my story?*

It was such a hellish way to live, but I thought it would pass. I still thought I could turn things around without really changing anything.

That conversation with Jason happened in late 2012. By early 2013, I'd left the company where he and I worked together and was set to start a new position at a bigger agency with a bigger title. I had my reasons for wanting to leave, but what

I wouldn't have admitted is that they'd all seen too much. I'd given several humiliating displays at company parties and, after the last incident, had been sat down by the partners. It was a kind, concerned, but very clear "this can't happen again" conversation — pretty much my worst work nightmare, aside from actually being fired (though at the time, I almost wished they had let me go).

Again, I made the problems about them. I overemphasized issues with my position and the company that were real but not as significant as I made them out to be. I didn't do this loudly, or openly, or spitefully, but I did it nonetheless. It's only now writing this that I can see what I was really doing: lying to myself so I wouldn't have to change. If I stayed, I would have faced too many mirrors reflecting back a truth I wasn't ready to face.

The reckoning came quickly enough, anyway. That spring, I got my DUI. Two months later was my brother's wedding.

Honesty has not come easily or quickly. I still have to work on it every day. It seems as though being honest would be a matter of a decision, like turning on a light. But my relationship with the truth was so distorted — I didn't even know what the truth fucking *was* — so it's been much more of a slow emergence from the dark.

Getting clean about drinking was just the start. It sounds absurd, but in that year I spent in purgatory between my brother's wedding and finally stopping, I still had this basic disconnect between what I thought and what I was actually *doing*. I knew there was nothing left for me in drinking; I knew that it was over and sobriety was the only option for me unless I was willing to lose Alma, along with everything else. I had accumulated so much knowledge, had read all the books, could recite the AA preamble and quote all kinds of profound literature about the boldness and courage and realities of sobriety. I had immersed myself so much in all of it, to the point that I believed I was *there*, when in reality I was still drinking every couple of weeks.

One piece of writing changed this. It is part of an essay in Augusten Burroughs's book *This Is How*, and I read it on my phone while walking home from the train one day. The words hit me so hard that I stopped and sat on a curb to finish, crouched over my phone, squinting to see through the glare the sun made on my screen. On that particular day, I was close to caving again.

He writes:

> In 100 percent of the documented cases of alcoholism worldwide, the people who recovered all shared one thing in common, no matter how they did it:
> They didn't do it.
> They just didn't do it.

By "it" he means drinking. They didn't drink.

It sounds so obvious, and it is. It's almost idiotic.

But this is where I was, and maybe it's where you are, too. At some point all the ideas and the beliefs and the good intentions and the reading and the planning and the "thinking about it" mean absolutely nothing if you're still doing the thing. I remember listening to a Marianne Williamson talk where she recounts a conversation she was having with a friend about their ambitions to get in shape. She says, and I'm paraphrasing, "Look, at some point, you're either going to the gym or you're not." The membership doesn't get you there. Your good intentions don't get you there. At some point, you actually have to show up to the gym.

The truth was, I wasn't going to the gym. Still drinking every few weeks was still drinking. If I wanted to stop drinking, I had to actually stop drinking.

Imagine that.

In my journal I have an entry from 2014 with two words: *One version*. Meaning, I wanted one version of me in the world, instead of the dozens there were. It felt light-years away, impossible, but it was the aim. I wanted it for many reasons, but primarily because I wanted to be able to write openly about this thing — drinking, sobriety, trying to get sober, all of it — and I knew I couldn't unless I stopped lying about where I stood.

So, the first step was to admit where I was in terms of days sober. I had to get clean with the people who could hold me accountable — and at that point, that meant my sponsor, a couple of people in AA, Holly, and Jon. He had called me out a few times in the months prior, noting inconsistencies in my behavior, and had outright asked if I had been drinking. I'd lied. He didn't buy it and had stopped wanting to see me as a result, and it crushed me.

I promised myself that if I drank again, I would say so immediately.

It's laughable how difficult this was for me. It's not as if I was the first person to drink after walking into their first AA meeting. There were people I knew who had been trying for years; people who drank again after decades of sobriety and came back; people I had become close to who would walk up and grab a twenty-four-hour chip at the end of the meeting after months of sobriety, seemingly so easily — and yet I just could not bring myself to come forward and just *say the words*. I was always fudging my truth by a little or a lot, depending on whom I was talking to.

Maybe it made sense to do this with Jake, or my parents, or friends who were worried about me — but with people in AA?! It was just so...*strange*. As Jason had said, "I see you do it all the time, even when you don't have to." All the dishonesty in my past was one thing, but to lie to sober people about sobriety was anathema.

I was so afraid of exposing myself as weak, dumb, or otherwise incompetent, even though no one else would see it that way. It's the reason I'd lied to every therapist I'd ever had — the reason I lied to anyone who could have ever helped me.

So the very first thing I did was get real there. It was excruciating. And yet it gave me something solid to stand on.

Then, I started practicing telling the truth, like I had seen and heard people do in meetings. I forced myself to raise my hand in every meeting, when before I never would. Every single time for at least a year, this made me sweat and shake. But every time I did it, I felt a little something in me release — a little, tiny piece of my twisted recording tape straightening out. At first, I just parroted others: using their phrases, modeling their ways of telling their story, until I could find my own way.

I can't express how much I despised doing this; it shattered my ego to pieces every goddamn time. I wanted to have a better story, a more congruent one, a way of stating it more eloquently and completely. I wanted to be able to speak without shaking or fumbling my words. I wanted to open my mouth without feeling like I was hurling myself off a cliff.

I also practiced with Jon. Although the romantic aspect of our relationship was volatile, there was also a real friendship underneath — a genuine affection and care. I remember one time early on, after he'd spent the night at my place, I woke up early in the morning with my heart pounding in my chest. As a reflexive response, I sat on top of him and began speaking. I told him everything: what had happened in college with Mike, what my relationships before Jake looked like, and then, everything that happened with Jake.

I left nothing out — I bared every detail, every motivation, all my manipulations, every ugly result. I told him about the other men I'd entangled myself with, including those I was still talking to. I told him things I'd told only a few of my closest friends and many things I'd never told anyone. I occasionally checked his expression, searching for signs of horror, but all I saw was evenness. Every so often he would gently nod, urging me to go on. I didn't cry. I didn't dramatize. I simply let it all spill out of me — a tumble of words, like a waterfall crashing onto his chest.

I think part of my motivation to out myself with Jon was selfish. I knew he found honesty sexy and refreshing, and he was so surprisingly honest himself — it was a large part of what attracted me to him. He was quick and enthusiastic to talk about anything, including his ambivalence about AA and sobriety, his own ugly past, his relationships, his family.

But I also wanted to level his view of me. I knew he liked me, and not just physically. I knew he liked and respected who I was. Although we had met through AA and thus he knew I was not exactly an angel, I wanted him to really know where I'd been and what kind of person he was lying next to.

Lying and withholding is the cheapest, easiest way to control others. You control their perception, control their response to you, control who you need them to be. In telling the truth, I was surrendering control with the hope that it would lead to something different. I hoped it would lead to something real.

I practiced being truthful with others, too. Mostly with the few women I knew from AA, including my sponsor. Often, with these women, it was an experiment. We'd be sitting there having a conversation like a tennis match. I'd be truth-telling with the best of them, and then — *whiz!* — a lie would escape out of my mouth. It was often something inane, like saying I'd been to a restaurant that I'd never been to, or that I read a book I hadn't.

I'd go, "Hold on! That was a lie! Where the hell did that come from?!" and we'd laugh. "Let me try again," I'd say, and I'd pick up the ball and begin again.

Sometimes I would tell ten lies in the course of an hour, but every time I'd call myself on it and feel a little better. Sometimes, I realized I'd lied only after I'd already gone home, and I'd force myself to call and say, "You know, I just have to out myself because it's bugging me — that thing I said? It wasn't true!" I learned to do this because other women did it with me, and I noticed they didn't vaporize — not when they told the truth, and not when they admitted to lying.

In July 2014, I started a new Instagram handle called @clear_eyes_full_heart. I did this separate from my original account because I wanted to be honest about sobriety without my friends and coworkers seeing. Through that account, I connected to an entire sober underworld I hadn't known existed, just by searching for hashtags like #sober and #sobriety.

It was through Instagram that I met Holly, who became the other half of the *HOME* podcast, a show we cohosted for almost three years; Becky, a dear friend with whom I've now cohosted several retreats and workshops; Meadow, who has become my ground and my West Coast lifeline; Elena, who has become a cherished teacher and friend; and so many others who changed my world. The online connections did not take the place of talking to people in real life or on the phone (I am now a very, very strong believer in the importance of actual face-to-face communication, far more so than I ever was then), but social media enabled many real connections to happen, and it provided me with a larger sense of community when I so desperately needed that.

Having that Instagram account did something else for me, too. It gave me a little playground to write and share things: little bits of my experience, photos, quotes I loved. And as small as it may sound, this was something I longed for more than anything in the world — sharing words.

I have always been a collector of words. I have dozens of journals, dating back to when I was nine years old, filled with quotes, passages from books, music lyrics, poems. For years, I ran a private Tumblr account called "On Blank," meaning "On [Subject]," where I collected and posted words that I thought best captured a specific sentiment or topic: "On Grief," "On Love," "On Tenderness," "On Missing Someone," "On Friendship." No one ever saw it (and I am kicking myself for deleting that thing now), but I loved doing it.

I'd started and stopped many blogs, mostly because I didn't post frequently enough or think I had enough to say, but now — now, I had something to write about. I had entire worlds to explore.

Around the same time, I created a blog called *I Fly at Night* and started publishing pieces there about what I was going through. I started doing this before I was even sober for good, and I wrote about my mistakes. It was a way of working through things when I couldn't speak the words out loud. No one was reading my blog then — people knew it existed only if I told them. Sometimes I would email a post to a small group of friends or share it with Jon or Holly or some of the other sober women I knew. I started slow, dipping my toe in. Writing, no matter how awkward and raw and poorly worded my posts were, began to stitch me together. Writing was healing me.

Sometimes I would unpublish a post out of fear of someone seeing — my parents, someone at work, or Jake — even though I wasn't necessarily saying anything implicating them. Then I would find the courage to republish it.

Eventually, I started to share my posts on Facebook and Instagram. Well-intentioned friends and family warned me that it might be dangerous to do that, since Jake and I were still not divorced, and what if something I wrote affected the custody agreement? Some asked if I was really sure I wanted to expose all that stuff, because what if I regretted it? Or what if I didn't stay sober? What if it tarnished my reputation at work, or ruined future job opportunities? What would Alma say if she read those things someday? People contacted my mom and asked if I was okay, since so much of what I wrote seemed to be "dark." Many in AA didn't agree with my breaking the principle of anonymity. I got a cease-and-desist letter from a lawyer, telling me to remove all references to someone I knew from AA; though I had never named her, she felt I described our relationship enough for it to be identifying.

Sometimes, these things gave me pause, but mostly they furthered my resolve. Ultimately, I wanted to be free more than I wanted to be safe. And writing was freeing me.

The effort of putting words to my experiences, of trying to describe things as accurately and precisely as possible, felt like it was saving my life. One sentence at a time, I was writing my way to an understanding and a grace I could not otherwise reach. With each word I wrote, I breathed power into a new story for myself and also slowly started to make sense of what I'd never been able to before.

Sometimes I still had trouble telling whether I was being deceitful in conversation or out in the world, but on the page it was painfully obvious. With writing, I could sit there and work through the words — erasing, writing, rewriting, mining for a more accurate way to express something until I reached it, until I captured the truth as closely as possible. I heard a famous author describe this once at a book reading. She said she appreciates writing so much because it's the place where she's the least full of shit.

Maybe writing doesn't call to you in the same way it did me, but I've come to believe there's great alchemical power in putting pen to paper for anyone. In every workshop, retreat, or class I teach, there is a writing element. In my online classes, I require students to adopt a "Morning Pages" practice, which was developed by Julia Cameron, author of *The Artist's Way*. She instructs you to do thirty minutes or three full pages of "automatic writing" each morning. Cameron herself is in recovery and found that this process was tremendously useful in not only clearing the subconscious but also boosting creativity. It's something I've now done for years, and I swear by it.

The trick is to allow yourself to write without editing your thoughts — to put down all the random, ugly, "unspiritual" junk, without worrying about punctuation, grammar, or content. You simply write what comes up and keep the pen moving until it's over. I think of it as taking out the trash.

Often, people worry that someone is going to find the pages, so they have trouble really being honest. In these cases, I tell them to burn or shred the pages afterward; the point is to get the words down, not to use the pages as an archive (mostly they are unintelligible, anyway, or at least mine are). My point is, there's something transformative about setting down on paper what's inside us. It clears out the junk so you can allow for a different transmission to come through. Sometimes, you find yourself in touch with a truth so powerful that it can point you in the right direction, or at least to the next step.

Many students have told me they've looked at journals from courses or workshops months or years ago and found they had "known what was true" long before it came to fruition in their lives — they saw it right there in their own words. I've seen the same in my journals. I wrote about being concerned about my drinking as far back as college — it is a theme in almost every entry for fifteen years — and yet I never verbalized it or spoke about it with anyone. All along, I knew.

I think there's a common misperception that people who are able to tell their story, who can talk about it publicly or even privately in some coherent, cogent manner, are gifted storytellers who do this naturally. I used to think that, while I was sitting in meetings or reading a memoir or hearing someone give a talk. But it is so much more a result of *practice* — a willingness to suck at something until you don't suck at it so much anymore.

Some of my earliest writings are incoherent and, frankly, awful. I've never listened to the hundreds of podcast episodes I've put into the world, but I'm positive that on more occasions than not I either was completely full of shit or else failed wildly to convey an intelligible point. But the *process* of creating all that work has changed me for the better. The process has been the gift.

As I progressed in my sobriety, I continued to reach points where I knew I had to approach a new layer of truth. This would usually come about because I'd start to experience enough emotional pain that I had no other choice. When my first and second sponsors both suggested that I embark on the steps, I always found a way to squirm out of it. Right when it got to step 4 — the part where you start to inventory the impacts of your behavior — I would magically get very busy.

Although I'd shared quite a lot of my story in my writing, on my podcast, in meetings, and with a few close friends, there were still people with whom I had not yet been willing or able to be fully honest. Publicly, withholding was necessary and right: there will always be parts of my life that are too private and sacred to share. But personally, it was a different matter. As time went on and the people closest to me got comfortable with my sobriety — as Jake, my close friends, and my family started to trust me and to have confidence that I was going to be all right — it would have been easy to just let the past slide away, unexamined. But I kept getting restless. I started to get angry, and in some cases overcome with rage. There were still a few relationships where I felt like a child, powerless to do anything but react and please. I couldn't speak up, because I was too afraid of the loss or the conflict, but I was also keenly aware that I could no longer hide in this way any longer. Not if I wanted to do what I knew I was capable of doing.

I kept repeating horrifically painful patterns with men, to the point of feeling worse than I had when I was drinking. I would obsess over men who treated me like shit, running through the same script over and over, repeating the same cycle of obsession and rejection, and feeling like I had absolutely no control over how I felt or what I did.

Around year three of sobriety, I reached an emotional bottom. I knew that if I kept going on as I had with men, I would eventually drink again. Through a string of serendipitous circumstances, I connected with Veronica, a sober woman I knew from my podcast and online sober communities. She had encountered the same sort of emotional bottom in her third year of sobriety and found someone who brought her through the twelve steps in a specific way, and she had "experienced a profound spiritual and emotional rearrangement as a result of that process." She offered to help me, and though I was entirely skeptical, I agreed.

Over the course of a few weeks, we worked together and went through the steps fully. She changed my perception of what the steps were. As ridiculous as it sounds, I hadn't quite grasped that the actual "program" of recovery in AA was the steps — not the fellowship, the meetings, or anything else. She walked me through things in a very tactical, practical, matter-of-fact way, and for the very first time I saw patterns in myself that I'd never been willing or able to see. Chiefly, that almost all the difficulty and pain I'd experienced in my relationships was rooted in a fundamental dishonesty on my part.

Again, I'd never thought I was an inherently dishonest person. People who lie are malevolent, right? Evil? Sociopathic or otherwise pathological? I could certainly recognize my outright lies and deception, but I hadn't seen the other ways in which I behaved, communicated, or otherwise represented myself dishonestly in relationships. Things like approval seeking, people-pleasing, not voicing my opinions, and avoiding conflict at any cost — *these were all dishonesty masked as something sweeter and more socially acceptable.*

I was pretty leveled by this. The work we'd done together was all laid out on paper, in my own handwriting. I could see the pattern laid out so obviously, so *simply*, in almost every difficult relationship I'd had — with everyone from childhood friends, to various girlfriends, to my parents, to certain coworkers, to almost every man I'd ever thought rejected me. At some point in the relationship, usually early on, I started to withhold my true thoughts and feelings, to slightly manipulate, to play chameleon in order to get them to see me in a certain way or to not upset them or to smooth things over so we could be closer.

I pretended not to be bothered by things that bothered me. I overextended myself. I acted like I wanted things I did not want. I said no when I meant yes, and yes when I meant no. I took responsibility for other people's feelings and for their lives. I anticipated their needs. I protected them, often by sacrificing myself. Fuck, I even pretended to like people I actually didn't like, because I either was afraid of them or thought I needed them on my side to be okay.

I basically tricked people into meeting my needs, and I called it being *kind*, being *nice*, being *easygoing* and *loving*, all the while growing increasingly resentful and spiteful until eventually — and inevitably — I would erupt and blow them out of my life forever.

This may sound like something excruciating to see in yourself, and it was. It certainly lifted a lot of the blame I had placed on others, which I found quite…*annoying*. But it also gave me back my power in places where I had felt utterly powerless. By seeing that I was not just a victim to the whims of other people and their seemingly shitty personalities and temperaments but that I had played an active part in a lot of my own pain, I had the chance to stop repeating the same mistakes. It was also — it *is* also — so critical that we know: all the things we do, every maladaptive behavior or pattern we have, is the result of a coping mechanism we learned in order to keep us alive or help us survive.

I wasn't deceiving people because I was a piece of shit; I was doing what I had learned to do as a child to survive. And I was doing what *worked*. It just wasn't — let's say — a superhealthy or productive way to operate as an adult.

Although dishonesty was the primary theme I uncovered, it wasn't the only thing I needed to face. I had put people in really difficult places as a result of my drinking, where they had to lie for me or take care of me and clean up messes that weren't theirs. I had selfishly dumped responsibilities that were mine onto others. I had used and manipulated people so I could get what I wanted, without much regard for them or their feelings. And then there was the worry — the never-ending worry people who loved me had to endure. The times my parents had to answer calls they shouldn't have had to answer, or my friends had to wonder where I'd gone and whether I was okay, or my brother had to wonder from two thousand miles away whether I was going to make it through a weekend, or even little Alma, who — despite being too young to consciously understand why — must have felt unsafe, unwatched, and afraid.

I can see this play out now sometimes with my friends. I can see the kids growing anxious when the drinking escalates. At a barbecue last summer, a bunch of families were watching a baseball game together, and my friend's nine-year-old brought her a glass of water and quietly asked her to stop drinking. I overheard. My friend wasn't outwardly drunk, but this is the thing: Kids have an inherent sense of danger and unease around alcohol because they know it makes us less *us*, less *there*. Even when it's normalized, even when nothing "bad" happens, they can feel it when our presence begins to slip away. They don't like it.

Alma can't name why I wasn't there at times, but she can point to very specific moments (and she does) when — even at the age of four or five — things weren't right. She still asks me questions like, "What happened? Where did you go?"

So what does one do with all this?

Through Veronica's gentle but firm guidance, I was instructed to take quick action on each of the relationships where I had harmed someone. Typically, this is done in the form of amends, and the amends process is something that is misunderstood outside of recovery circles and even within them. Amends are not meant to be you falling at the feet of everyone you've ever wronged and groveling, begging for forgiveness; nor are they an exhaustive confession of your sins. Amends are a very tactical, purposeful acknowledgment of the way your behavior may have affected someone, a general statement of your wrongdoings, and a commitment to proceed differently in the future.

I had successfully avoided amends for three years. I can't overstate how terrified I was of doing them. I didn't sleep. I wrote them out again and again. I did my best to make excuses and delay. But I kept reminding myself of what I already knew to be true: eventually, you just have to jump off the damn cliff.

By and large, my amends went well. I made them with friends, family, and a few of my old coworkers. I was mostly met with grace and tenderness and, in some cases, surprise that I had thought it necessary to make them.

Jake came last. His was the hardest.

When I sat down with him, it wasn't to recount the events of our past, blow by blow, but to explicitly acknowledge, for the first time, the deep regret for the pain and damage I had caused. To our relationship, to our family, and to him.

It was to say the words:

I loved you, but not well.

I am sorry.

I will do better.

Until then, he and I had never talked specifically about a lot of what had happened between us. Once we split up, the hacking away at each other largely ended, and we turned to handling ourselves individually, with our own support networks. Things between us then were calm — we had established a good co-parenting rapport and had leaned on each other as friends from time to time — but I had still been carrying a heavy burden of blame and sadness in my heart.

I read the words I had written to him (I didn't trust I'd make it through otherwise) and glanced up when I could, to gauge him. I don't know what I expected, but all I saw in his eyes was a neutral kindness. I saw the boy I had once loved with such ease, before we'd gone through our war. And maybe a flash of acknowledgment of the girl he had once known, too — the basic tenderness at the center of our story.

He thanked me, and we went our separate ways.

I don't know what that conversation meant to him, but it was gold to me. When I left the coffee shop afterward, I cried the coolest tears of relief. I hadn't realized just *how* heavy the weight had been, how severely I had desired the explicit acknowledgment of his mercy. For so long — for years — there had been an imbalance of power between us. He was the hero, and I the villain. I the child, and he the adult. I had been tiptoeing and sidestepping in all our conversations and interactions — hypervigilantly trying to avoid the land mines of our past. And in that way, I was frozen in time. Maybe he had been, too; I don't know.

I walked back home thinking about how, when we were in the worst of our days and I'd pulverized both of our hearts and couldn't make sense of what I was doing or stop, I would constantly pray that one day things would just be okay. *Just okay. Please. Just let us be okay. And if we can't both be okay, then just let him be.*

I knew then that I didn't have to settle for *okay* anymore. He was better than *okay*, and I was allowed to be, too.

What I want you to take away from this is not that you must do amends, but that — if you truly want to live with peace in your heart and be free of the burdens of the past — you must be brave enough to be willing to look at yourself honestly, clearly, and without reservation. You must take responsibility for everything that's ever happened to you. Not blame. *Responsibility.* There are, of course, parts of your life that simply can't be your fault. You could not control much of what happened to you as a child, for example, or whether you were abused or raped or have a chronic illness, so to say you have a part in anything like that would be untrue and damaging. But you can decide — by no longer allowing the circumstances of your life to victimize you — that none of it owns you anymore. You can say, *Now, I know better. Now, I know different. I am not helpless anymore.* And then you can go about doing the hard work of healing.

This is the singular, hard truth I come up against every day: *I am the only one responsible for my experience.*

I decide what I let in; I decide who I let in; I decide how to perceive things; I choose it all. If I start to believe differently, I suffer. This is not something I made up. It was taught to me. Not just in words but in the lives of the people I most admire. It was shown to me by Veronica, who learned it from the ones who went before her, who learned from the ones who went before them. And it is, in my experience, the primary difference between those who recover and those who don't.

People who stay sick choose to keep blaming. They stand firmly in their anger and resentment and call it a revolution. They bristle against this kind of work because they view it as an affront to their sovereignty. They don't see that humility is not an admission of weakness but a result of knowing exactly how powerful you are.

It's much easier to go down the path of self-righteousness, to be sure. Nothing is more gratifying. I fall into it regularly. But those who choose the other way?

They get better.

They get free.

They soar, with soft dignity. They rise, without needing to announce it.

What I know is this: The truth is ultimately life affirming. Even when it is ugly and inconvenient and has the potential to dismantle your life. It feels like relief even when it's painful. And call it my pseudoscientific woo-woo explanation, but I believe this is because the energy of truth is in integrity with the energy of the Divine. Not in a "this is good and now you're not bad" way but in a "this is real and therefore you can stand on it" way. The truth is uncomfortable but expansive. Lying is uncomfortable but confining. You know the difference when you feel it.

For most of my life I believed I had to lie to get what I needed. I'm guessing somewhere inside, you believe this, too. But I had it wrong — and so do you. While lying *almost* works, just like drinking *almost* works, neither will ever take us all the way home. While the path may be longer and harder and a little lonelier at times, honesty will always move you closer to love, not further away.

Today I don't walk around looking over my shoulder, afraid of being found out. I don't fear picking up my phone or looking at texts or opening my mail. I don't protect different versions of myself, and I don't have to keep track of my stories, because there aren't any — there's just the one life I'm living.

I'll never forget the day it hit me that things were altogether different. It was a lazy Sunday afternoon in July a couple of years ago. Alma had just come back from Jake's. They'd been at the beach, so I sent her into the shower, and afterward, she crawled into my bed to watch a show. The breeze was blowing through my room, making the curtains toss little orbs of light on my bed. I had a stinky trash bag in one hand and an unpeeled carrot in the other as I peeked into the room to tell her I was taking out the trash and then getting a Diet Coke down the street. She nodded, already engrossed in the show. I walked out and threw the trash into the bin, and a bunch of flies spun up toward my face. As I walked down the driveway, the sun hit my eyes, and I took a big bite of the carrot. My mind started to wander, searching for the familiar grooves of worry or scheming or protection to run down, but there wasn't anything there but smooth spaciousness. There was the warm sun making rainbows behind my eyelids and my bare feet hitting the baking asphalt and a bit of chewed-up carrot in my mouth.

I had nothing left to hide.

II

Burning Lonely

Stand still. The trees ahead and bushes beside you
Are not lost. Wherever you are is called Here,
And you must treat it as a powerful stranger,
Must ask permission to know it and be known.
The forest breathes. Listen. It answers,
I have made this place around you.
If you leave it, you may come back again, saying Here.
No two trees are the same to Raven.
No two branches are the same to Wren.
If what a tree or a bush does is lost on you,
You are surely lost. Stand still. The forest knows
Where you are. You must let it find you.

— DAVID WAGONER, "LOST"

This is a good time to talk about loneliness. Because sober or not, until you start to tell the truth, you're going to be desperately lonely. Perhaps this is obvious, but I'm pretty sure it escapes most of us.

We know we're lonely — it is no secret that loneliness is the great emotional epidemic of our time — but we don't really know *why*. I know that most of my life, I felt a nagging ache of separateness I could not name. Despite being surrounded by people, having a big social life, more plans than I had time for, and a solid group of people I considered friends, I still felt very much alone. I felt alone in my marriage. I felt alone in my friendships. And actually being alone by myself? Forget it — that was intolerable.

Drinking gave me the illusion of connection, though, so when I was drinking with people, as I said before, I felt like we were getting closer. I felt like alcohol allowed us to break down barriers, to slide closer to our truer selves and to each other, closer than we could ever get without it. But when the buzz wore off, the separateness returned, and often it was intensely magnified.

Naturally, then, when I stopped drinking — and this is something I hear almost universally — I felt a loneliness like never before. There is a literal aspect to this: You left the proverbial island. All your friends live there, in that place, and you are actually going off into the unknown, away from the people and places and things that used to comfort you and catch you. But there's also the *visceral* aspect. Even if the connection was artificial — the connection I felt to other people through drinking, and the way I felt connected to myself, too — now that connection was gone. So even when I was with people, I had no idea how to connect to them. I would have never considered most of my relationships to be based on drinking, but when I started to get sober, I realized that most of them — probably 95 percent — were. Even the ones that weren't took time to recalibrate.

Although it sucked, at least it made sense: of *course* I was lonely. My entire social circle had fallen away. But I didn't realize it was deeper than that — so much deeper. Because the loneliness didn't end when I started to know people in sobriety or when I found new ways to fill my time. Loneliness started to abate only when I began to really let people in and tell them the truth, and that took a long, long time.

The antidote to loneliness wasn't just being around others or sharing common ground. It was intimacy.

My friend Meadow's definition of intimacy is the best one

I've heard. She says, "Intimacy is having a kind, compassionate witness to your truest thoughts and feelings."

A kind, compassionate witness

to

your truest thoughts and feelings.

Had I ever had anything like that? Have you?

For me, the answer was no. And not for lack of people who wanted to be there for me; there had always been — even in my darkest days — people who simply wanted to love me for who I was, and who did. My mom and my brother, for example. But I couldn't let them, or anyone else, come anywhere near that close. I didn't know how. I didn't want to.

Most of us don't, even though we say we do.

Because this is the thing: intimacy requires getting really comfortable with fear, all the time. It requires surrendering your ego, and all the illusions you have about yourself, and often the illusions others have about you, too. Worse than that, intimacy means that you risk loving, which is the scariest enterprise, because the degree to which your heart expands in love is the degree to which you risk the pain of losing it.

Having a witness also means being seen. Really seen. In all our humanity — flaws and ugly bits and all. Even the most courageous of us are willing to go about 90 percent of the way there, but we hold on to that last 10 percent, the part that could allow us to *really* be known. Sobriety hasn't so much been about revealing the 90 percent but that last 10. The little bit I always want to keep for myself.

The problem is, 10 percent of withholding, or secretiveness, will still eventually contaminate the whole. Having 10 percent of your blood infected, or 10 percent of the cells in your pinkie toe be cancerous, is enough to make you terminally ill and eventually kill you. And keeping 10 percent of yourself from your partner, or whomever you could trust with your heart, will make you 100 percent lonely.

Let me give you an example: A friend of mine went on a date with a guy, their first, and while they were waiting for their food to arrive, a song came on that she loves. She said, "Oh, I love this song!" Her date immediately echoed back, "Ohh, me too! They're great," so my friend got excited. A little later, she asked him if he'd seen the band play at the House of Blues in their town last year, to which her date responded, "Who?"

My friend ignored the response. She acted like she didn't hear him; she told herself it didn't matter that he lied, that it wasn't a big deal, anyway — it was just a stupid song. Why? Because she wanted it to work. She wanted him to like her. She wanted to be agreeable. She wanted to not feel so alone anymore and to not feel the same heartbreak of trying things and having them "not work out" over and over and over again.

This is the 10 percent withholding. It doesn't seem like a big deal, but right then they agreed it was okay to lie to each other — even if only just a little. She agreed not to look *too* closely, and he agreed to the same. They proceeded into a full-blown relationship after that, living together and all. But they were always operating just left of center, hovering around the truth of who they were, unwilling to lift the film from their eyes.

It was a lot safer this way, but it was also extraordinarily lonely, and ultimately, a few years later, she left.

This is what I mean. It would have been a risk to call him out on the little fudging of the truth. Even if it had just been an innocent misunderstanding or he had been trying to impress her, she would have had to withstand a moment of discomfort. It might have ruined the date. Or — *or* — it might have allowed them to actually find an honest ground zero from which to build something. Denying that 10 percent meant she didn't have to be alone for the next few hours, but it also ensured she would stay lonely for the next few years, because in that moment they silently agreed to something.

We can begin with ourselves.

The first time I tried to meditate, I shook uncontrollably. I was in my late twenties, recently married, and had signed up for a forty-day yoga program at the Baptiste yoga studio in Cambridge. Part of the protocol was to practice meditating for ten minutes each day.

I thought it would be simple enough, but I was also the person who'd never been able to make it through savasana pose at the end of yoga practice. I figured it was a pointless, extra part of the class. We were just lying there. Doing nothing. *What for?*

A couple of times I tried, and the stillness was so uncomfortable — my mind would race, strange sensations would arise in my body, or I would start to feel like I was going to cry or scream out of nowhere — so I said "screw that." From there on out, when the teacher cued us to get into that resting pose at the end of class, I took that as my cue to roll up my mat and head out.

When I tried to meditate, things were not all that different. I set myself up with a couch cushion on the floor in our office. The birds were chirping outside. I sat up straight, cross-legged, closed my eyes, and set my hands on my legs the way the teacher had instructed us. My arms immediately started shaking — literally bouncing off my thighs. My eyelids wouldn't stay shut; the harder I worked to close them, the stronger they flitted up and open. Then my thighs started to twitch. I kept trying, kept imagining the ocean or focusing on my breath like she had told us to do, but it only seemed to make things worse.

I had that same urge to cry or scream that I did in savasana. *What the fuck!* I thought. After a couple of minutes — probably even less — I gave up. I didn't try again for years. I figured I'd stick to the *moving* kinds of meditation: running, walking, vigorous yoga, that kind of thing.

How I felt in those few minutes of trying to meditate is more or less what I felt like *all the time* in early sobriety. I found other ways to soothe and medicate myself, like ice cream, men, endlessly scrolling on social media, and Netflix binges (all of which were far better than drinking, because they weren't going to kill me or cause me to kill someone else), but eventually I still had to learn how to be with myself.

On Thanksgiving in my first year of sobriety, Jon and I were in an "on" phase of our relationship. Alma was spending the holiday with Jake that year, so Jon came with me to my mom's friend's house for dinner, and then we spent the following two days together. On Sunday morning, I started to get anxious and antsy, anticipating that he would be heading home soon and I'd be alone. I hid this, of course, knowing how clingy and needy it would seem — we'd just spent three consecutive days together without any break. It was perfectly normal for him to want to go home to his own space, to do his own thing.

It was out of character for me, too. I'd always prided myself on being independent in my relationships.

After we had breakfast, he went to check train schedules, signaling that it was almost time for him to leave. My mind started to race with what I could do with myself once he was gone, but there was nothing. Most of my old relationships had fallen off by then, and the ones that existed were too new for a Sunday-afternoon hangout. I could go to a meeting, but the idea of that just made me feel worse.

Jon mentioned that he was going to watch football with some of his friends who were out in the city.

"You're going to go out drinking, aren't you?" I asked, already knowing.

"I don't know, Laura. Maybe. But if I do, I'm not doing that *at* you. I mostly just need to go home."

When he left, I spent a while flaying him in my mind, thinking about what a shitty dickface he was for leaving. How disrespectful he was to me, to my sobriety. That he could have lied about the drinking part, at least. That I probably shouldn't even be with him. Then I spent another long while feeling sorry for myself. Because yet again, there was nowhere for me to be. I belonged to no one, nowhere. I got myself dressed to go on a run, thinking I would burn it out of me.

With layers of winter running gear, a heavy coat, a hat, and gloves on, I went searching for my headphones. I found them lodged between the cushions of my couch, and when I went to plug them into my phone, I gasped suddenly, like I'd been punched in the chest.

All the energy drained out of me. I started to cry.

I realized there was no amount of running, or drinking, or anything that could hold off what was coming, what I had been trying to stop for so long — the crushing blow of loneliness.

Piece by piece, I took off my layers: coat, sweatshirt, neck warmer, hat, gloves, shoes, socks. Then I got down on all fours and sprawled onto the floor, until I was belly-down on my rug like a starfish. I told myself to try, just try, dropping all the stories I had about what was going on — like I had heard my teachers talk about — and to instead just focus on the sensations in my body.

The stories kept hammering at me, serving up their long list of evidence and proof of how alone I was, how alone I would always be. I would complete one breath without a story, and then another one would surface, and I would bring myself back, and then another would show up. For a while, the pain got worse, and my mind raced faster — much worse, much faster.

As for my body, there was a physical ache in my chest, like my rib cage was being pried apart, and it intensified every time I inhaled. I searched for the color and the temperature and the shape of what I was feeling, like I had learned in so many talks and books: *red, hot, stinging, fast*. I focused on those things instead of the stories my mind was telling me. I tried to stay present to just the sensations themselves and to each single breath.

Gradually, very gradually, all the spinning stories and cruel thoughts began to slow. They slowed, and slowed, and slowed, until I had only one thought left, and I realized I'd been whispering it to myself.

Sweet girl, you're okay.
Sweet girl, you're okay.
Sweet girl, you're okay.

After a little while, a pristine stillness filled the room. I could hear the heat clicking through the walls. Tears were running down my face sideways onto the scratchy rug, and I could see fibers from it dance around in a faint beam of bruised light coming through the window, the last whimper of the day. A car passed by on the wet road.

I was still there.

I wasn't any of those stories I had been telling myself; I was just a girl lying on a rug feeling something. By herself, but not alone. I had witnessed her. She had been witnessed. This might have been the first time I experienced true intimacy — the first of so many since then. And I realized: this was possible for me. Not only possible. It was *probable*.

Perhaps this was what it was like to be in love. Perhaps it started with me.

What I did that day was part instinct, part an accumulation of everything I'd learned and read and seen others do, and part grace. It was simple, incredibly difficult, and one of the most exquisite, life-giving things you can ever learn to do: to witness yourself, without judgment, as you struggle to stay.

How many times had I berated myself for what I felt that day? How many times had I drank at those feelings or even the slightest hint that they might be coming? How many times had I run, numbed, lied, ate, scrolled, drugged, slept, screamed, or otherwise avoided them? Hundreds. Thousands. But all it took was that one time — the one good try — to show me what it was like to ride it out instead. To be her friend, instead of her enemy. To love her like I would Alma, instead of beating the shit out of her again.

The strangest thing happened then, too. In the quiet space that filled in once the storm had passed, there was a presence. I can't explain this any way other than to say I was witnessing, but that I was also being witnessed. And held. I was both.

I don't know a whole lot of the Bible, but I do have a favorite passage, from Luke 15:31. It says, "You are always with me, and everything I have is yours." It comes from the parable of the prodigal son. In the story, a father has two sons. The younger son asks his father for his inheritance early, and then leaves home and squanders his fortune. He eventually becomes impoverished and is forced to return home, empty-handed, and intends to beg his father to accept him as a servant. To his surprise, he's received by his father with open arms and is celebrated. The older son, who has obeyed his father all his life, is angry and refuses to participate in the festivities. The father tells the older son, "You are always with me, and everything I have is yours."

Although this is a story about love and redemption and mercy, it is also the essence of everything I want you to hear about loneliness.

You are always with me. You are never alone.

And everything I have is yours. You are granted all the love in the universe simply because you exist, not because you are good. Love was never yours to lose — you cannot lose it. It will never let you go.

What this all boils down to, I think, is a message of belonging. To a love bigger than anything you could possibly fathom on your own. An impossible, intractable love. An indestructible one that exists inside you. Right now. *Always.*

I have learned, and I keep learning, to be a kinder witness to myself, first. Some moments are harder than others, because some aspects of myself are far more difficult to face than others. Like weakness. Like neediness. Like jealousy. But I practice, and I am reminded, and I continue to try. Over the years, being alone with myself — especially in meditation — has become something I crave and appreciate, rather than something I fear and avoid. Not always, but more often.

Then, of course, there is the part of intimacy that involves others.

If you were reading my friend Meadow's definition of intimacy earlier and thought, *I don't have anyone or anything like that in my life*, it is okay.

I asked for people to show up for me. As in, I prayed for it. I prayed for teachers and friends, and I still pray for a partner. Over time, people have appeared. You don't need a whole crew of them — just one is perfect. And then another. And then maybe another. I found them in AA in the early days; I found them through the new work I started to do writing and teaching; I found them because I got healthier, and as I did, I attracted people who were different — healthier themselves and thus capable of entrusting and being trustworthy with my heart.

But I have had to be willing to risk myself — and you will, too. I've often hoped people would just show up at my door, but so far that has not happened. I've had to get off my phone and my computer, and go out into the world. I've had to extend myself and risk rejection, and I've had to learn to sit in the space between — when there was no one, and no thing — and to trust that the space was important and necessary.

In David Whyte's poem "The House of Belonging," he writes:

This is the temple
of my adult aloneness
and I belong
to that aloneness
as I belong to my life.

There is no house
like the house of belonging.

I can't tell you how many times I have whispered these words to myself. *This is the temple of my adult aloneness.*

We think it is the aloneness we fear, but I believe what we actually fear is not having a home within ourselves. For so long, I did not trust my own landscape. I had believed the stories I learned about it, and I had taken every chance to avoid living there, and learning *her*. Sobriety forced a closeness to myself and to life that was at first excruciating. It burned, and it burned, and it burned. But in the ashes from burning all the things I was not, I found her. I found me.

And then I could finally be found by others.

12

We Are All
Magnificent Monsters

*The great epochs of our life come when we gain the courage
to rechristen our evil as what is best in us.*

— Friedrich Nietzsche, *Beyond Good and Evil*

Last year the man I was dating got approached by one of his
friends. His friend casually but not so casually asked if he
was seeing someone, because that was the word around town.
My boyfriend confirmed that yes, he was indeed Seeing Someone. The friend warned him that he might want to be careful
about the company he keeps.

Apparently, the words that followed were: "Word from the
rumor mill is, she's a raging alcoholic who cheated on her husband and lost custody of her daughter. Not sure you want to
associate yourself with people like that."

A raging alcoholic.

Who cheated on her husband.

And lost custody of her daughter.

Huh.

My first reaction, naturally, was to get defensive. I wanted to retaliate, burn their shit down, and set the record straight. I live in a pretty small town. Were these the same people I exchanged smiles and pleasantries with at school pickups, soccer games, or the grocery store? Or were they ones who knew me even better than that?

After a short while, the anger seeped out of me. Because this was the reality of my life on that day: I'd been sober for over four years. It had been a long time since I had raged, or anything close to it. My daughter (whom I never lost custody of) was at school, where I'd dropped her off that morning. Around three o'clock, I would pick her up, as I did every day, because I no longer worked at a marketing agency in the city but for myself. I'd worked my ass off to carve out a new career writing, teaching, and speaking.

Earlier that day, I'd taught eighty people about how to work with grief in early sobriety. And the husband? Even in the worst of times, that was never our bottom-line story. We were always so much more than that.

The real irony was, I'd been talking about my story publicly for years. There was no need for the rumor mill. All the gossip was right there, plain as day, written out on my blog and documented in hundreds of hours of podcasts. The story wasn't about me, not really.

The reason I'm sharing this story with you is not because I want you to know what assholes people can be but because I want you to see that most of the time other people's perceptions of you have nothing to do with you. Yes, I wanted to judge the hell out of those people, and I nursed more than one fantasy about approaching them in the midst of one of the rumor mill parties and going all *Pretty Woman* on them: "*Big* mistake. *Big. Huge!*" But it didn't take too long for me to find a long line of evidence of the same behavior in myself. The truth is, this is just what we do. It's what humans do when we feel small, which is often. We judge and we minimize and we assume and we talk about other people, because it's the cheapest form of social currency and connection, and because it's a hell of a lot easier than looking at ourselves.

Also?

There was *some* truth to it...it wasn't a story pulled out of thin air. But even in my darkest days, when I was still drinking and acting like a complete jerk, that story wasn't the whole one. It certainly wasn't the truest one.

The truest story — the one that will *always* be truest — is that I am a human being, being human. Sometimes, I am my best self. Sometimes, not so much. But goddamn, I am trying to do better. I am always trying to do better. My guess is that you are, too.

Of course, I wouldn't have always had this perspective. At one time hearing something like this would have leveled me completely. I would have spiraled, hidden myself away, and done anything to unhear those words. I had worked my entire life to try to shape your opinion of me, and to avoid — at any and all costs — criticism and judgment far less than what I'd heard that day. Why? Because I was ashamed.

Ashamed of my body.

Ashamed of my feelings.

Ashamed of my desire to be loved.

Ashamed of my attempts to "get it."

I was ashamed long before I had any reason to be.

And then, eventually, I had reasons to be.

I was ashamed of my drinking.

I was ashamed of all the places it brought me.

I was ashamed of who I'd become in my marriage.

I was ashamed of who I was as a mother.

I was ashamed of who I was as a friend.

I was ashamed.

Until a few years ago, I would have had no defense against those words from the rumor mill. But when I heard them that day, I did. On that day, I had already looked every one of my worst nightmares straight in the face. I had already turned over every shameful part of me, like rocks on a muddy beach. And I had decided — instead of casting them back into the sea, or smashing them, or trying to bury them out of existence — I would treat them as if they were holy. I would treat every part of me that way.

I had looked at each mistake and ugly part of my past up close; examined every crack and mineral and texture; and then held it in my palms, washed it clean, kissed it, and set it back down. I did this because I realized there was no amount of self-denigration or punishment that would keep those rocks from coming back to shore, anyway. So rather than try to banish half of me or more, I decided to invite it all in.

I decided to make a home for myself, inside myself. In the dirty, cracked mess of me. I decided to love it all.

You may be nodding because you're already there. You get it. Or else you may be wondering *how — how exactly do you get there?*

You can't imagine looking at your past — or all of yourself — without flinching, let alone finding a way to love it. You can't imagine being free from the shame and guilt and regret.

Many of the answers as to how I've already talked about: Pushing off from here. Treating yourself with the same care and priority as you would a growing life. Taking steps to tell the truth — if only, at first, by listening to other people tell theirs. Sitting with yourself through a moment of anger or jealousy or grief and just observing, as best you can, as a compassionate witness. Believing — if only because I'm telling you to — that there are thousands of other hearts out there who have ached in the exact same way, and that they've found a way to wholeness one breath at a time. Believing me when I tell you that you will not be left out of the miracle if you keep going.

But there's another piece. And I really, really want you to hear this.

You are a human. Not an addict, or an alcoholic, or any of the worst things you've ever done. Addiction is just an experience, one of many that can shape a life. It's not unique. It's not a flaw. It's not even that interesting. It's a natural human instinct — to soothe, to connect, to experience ourselves differently — gone awry. It's one of the fundamental aspects of our nature, written into every religious and anthropological record from the beginning of time.

The only thing it says about you or me is that we are a human just like all the other humans who have ever existed. That's it.

But, you say, *that's not how other people see it.* And you're right. People largely misunderstand addiction, and some people — no matter what you say or do or how loudly or for how long — will never really get it. As I've illustrated, there will always be people at the rumor mill slinging stories. So you could spend all your precious time trying to fight that fact, or you could see that none of it has anything to do with you and instead decide to keep building a life *you* really want to live. You could write a story you really fucking love.

Now obviously, not everyone experiences addiction to the degree that I did or that perhaps you did or still are. My thing happened to be alcohol. I don't know why. I don't even *care* why. It just is — or it was — the thing that broke me, and thank God for that. Because I see it now as my personal invitation. This weird, curious condition where ingesting a liquid substance (you really have to think about it like that sometimes, because it is just so *odd*) has profound physical, psychological, and spiritual effects on me to the point that I organized my entire life around it and nearly allowed it to kill me. Really? It's so weird!

But, also, a total gift. It was my opening. It led me straight to everything I had always wanted but never knew how to get. And it *had* to break me. There was no other way. There is no other way for any of us.

Johann Wolfgang von Goethe wrote in his poem "The Holy Longing":

And so long as you haven't experienced
This: to die and so to grow,
You are only a troubled guest
On the dark earth.

Before I went through all this, I was only a troubled guest. I was caught up with trying to be good, or else hating the ways in which I was bad. And I saw only those things in others, too: good, bad; right, wrong. It was a painful, shallow existence. It was Groundhog Day at the rumor mill.

These days I honestly don't sit around wondering if people are bad or good. I already know they are both. I can't say I'm perfect, or perfectly without judgment, but I'm telling you the truth when I say there is so much more space for compassion inside me. For other people and often — though not as easily — for myself. And in that space, good things have grown. Interesting, layered things.

I remember sitting in meetings very early on, hearing people share, and knowing for the first time in my life — not reading about, or listening to, or thinking about, but actually *knowing* — what it was like to suffer. I thought, *These people are* actual *heroes.*

So much of what I'd perceived to be courageous or successful or important or interesting had been such a joke up until then. I hadn't known anything about life at all: what it meant to meet your limitations or the depths of your capacity for pain, or how hard it was to actually change. I had judged people. I had laughed at their weaknesses. I had thought myself better in a thousand ways, immune to the circumstances and situations that create the realities we live in.

But those early meetings, and the daily struggle of that first year or so, stripped away most of my illusions. It was like being introduced to an underworld, a much deeper layer of the human experience, and it didn't take me long to see that it was the place I'd always been chasing. It just looked a hell of a lot different than I'd thought it would, and the price I had to pay to get there was far more than I expected.

In this world, my mistakes are as sacred as my triumphs. In this world, the ugly and the dazzling are the same. In this world, there is room for both joy and terror, pleasure and pain. In this world, nothing is too shameful to speak of. Nothing counts you out.

In this world, I am already, and always, forgiven. And so are you.

We are all magnificent monsters, capable of everything — all the light and every bit of the dark. Only some of us know this. We get to walk as humble guests, not troubled ones, with our feet in the mud and our hearts stretched toward the sky. Part earth, part heaven. We don't fear hell, because we've already been there, so our only promise is to keep going — to try to do a little bit better in this moment than we did in the last. And we know that is enough.

13

The Wrong
Damn Question

*It ain't what you don't know that gets you into trouble.
It's what you know for sure that just ain't so.*

— attributed to Mark Twain

I used to take the Quiz. You know, the "Am I an Alcoholic?" one — with twenty questions promising to reveal whether or not you should stop what you're doing and head to a 12-step meeting.

I took it in my twenties and, to my relief, answered "no" to enough questions. I took it again in my thirties and stopped answering around question 5 — "Have you given up hobbies or activities you used to enjoy?" — because I thought that was stupid. *Of course I've given up hobbies and activities I used to enjoy — I have a toddler.*

Maybe you've never taken the quiz, or maybe you have. I know my in-box is full of emails from people who are asking themselves the same questions that quiz asked me. And their answers pulse with the same level of unnecessary detail and caveats I used to mutter at my computer screen.

I'm going to offer a completely different alternative. This suggestion is likely to make some very smart and well-meaning heads explode, but it's a question worth asking if we're ever going to really change how we view this stuff.

Who cares if you're an alcoholic?

Honestly. Who cares? What would it mean if I told you that you were? What would it mean if I told you you were not?

Let's play out each scenario:

Scenario 1: Yes, You Are an Alcoholic

Congratulations, you've acquired an unwanted label! Instead of feeling empowered to explore your relationship with alcohol with openness and curiosity, it becomes *a thing*. It means you possibly have to...what? Seek support? Go to a 12-step meeting? Confess your condition to your friends and family?

And now suddenly changing your relationship with alcohol — which could have been a positive choice you make for yourself — now becomes an impossible chore, a "broken piece" in you that you have to "fix," a standard for judging yourself and others. Your perspective shifts from *How can I take the best care of myself possible, so I can feel connected and alive in my life?* to feeling jealous and comparing yourself with others who are "not alcoholics" and "get" to drink "normally."

Now maybe, you don't mind taking on the label *alcoholic* because it gives you a real reason to abstain from drinking. It's cold, hard proof you can show your friends and family and co-workers when they ask why you're not having wine with dinner.

"Oh, I can't do that anymore," you say, as you pull your alcoholic ID card from your wallet and lay it on the table with a satisfied smile, "I am an alcoholic." Kind of like turning down dessert because you're diabetic. Because what other reason is passable? You couldn't possibly just...choose *not* to drink. Shudder.

I'm making this scenario sound absurd because it is. Most people would rather be diagnosed with a personality disorder than alcoholism. What it really comes down to is this: Do you give yourself permission to make your own choices — choices that are good for you?

Scenario 2: No, You're Not an Alcoholic

You sigh with relief. *Thank God*, you think. *Now I can go back to drinking my wine without worrying that I'll soon find myself drinking vodka out of the bottle in my bathtub — just to keep from beating the kids.*

Maybe you skip the wine here and there because you remember how great you felt for that month and a half when you gave it up for Lent. Maybe you do a Dry July or a Sober October, and each time, you feel that same surprising sense of optimism and openness to life.

But you go back to alcohol because, well, you're not an *alcoholic*. Your spark dims a bit. That pesky anxiety gnaws at you. You're generally hazy and less motivated. But that's just life, right? You're not an alcoholic, so these feelings can't be related to the margarita you had last night. Alcohol's only real side effect is a hangover, right?

Besides, you can quit easily — whenever you want. What's two glasses of wine with dinner, anyway? Life is meant to be lived! *C'est la vie* and *carpe diem*! You've never suffered any negative consequences from drinking, really. You're not like the girl whose book you read, who crashed her car and got a DUI and left her daughter unattended during a blackout. Or the person who drank in the mornings, or the one who lost custody of his kids, or the one who lost his job because he called in sick too many days because he was hungover.

It's not like that.

It's fine.

You're *fine*.

It's not like you're an alcoholic.

See what I mean? The label means too much. Addiction is so stigmatized in our society that we think there are only two types of people when it comes to drinking: alcoholics and everyone else. And if you're not in the first bucket, drinking is fun! In fact, who would quit unless they *had* to?

One woman wrote me a letter describing how her mood and outlook improved after a month without wine, and — because feeling so much better surprised her — she was concerned she might be an alcoholic. As if only alcoholics feel better when they don't drink.

Being an alcoholic or not had no bearing on the anxiety and cravings she felt around dinnertime the first week she didn't drink. No, those cravings surfaced because alcohol is an addictive substance and a social buffer and she wasn't using it anymore. She'd become used to life with alcohol and had maybe even become addicted to it. *Because it's addictive.*

Here's the dirty little truth no one likes to admit — *everyone feels better in the long run when they don't drink*. Not just alcoholics — everyone. Because putting alcohol into your body isn't life giving; it's life sucking. Nobody's life actually *improves* because of alcohol, even though most people I know would scoff at that — *That's what* you *think* [*wink, wink* *clink, clink*] — and society tells us otherwise ten ways to Sunday.

Most people have no idea what their bodies feel like without it for an extended period of time. Alcohol is so normalized, so everywhere, so much a part of the fabric of mainstream society that most people will never experience life without it unless they're forced to.

Weird, right?

Isn't it completely fucking bizarre that we don't question (and, in fact, highly encourage) regular consumption of a drug that's more harmful and causes more deaths than cocaine, heroin, and meth combined? If someone stopped doing coke for a month and felt better, we wouldn't sit there and wonder whether they were an addict or could go back to recreational line snorting. Or let's look at smoking, which we were duped for decades into thinking was actually fine, and even healthy! Now that we know better, nobody questions the decision to stop smoking. Smoking is just so obviously stupid and dangerous.

And yet, alcohol is still cool. Unless you're an alcoholic. In which case you'd better deal with it...

...quietly...

...over there...

...without ruining the party for everyone else.

I have a friend who loves to drink. When we used to hang out, he'd have five or six beers in one sitting...at lunch. (I joined in gladly, relieved I didn't have to be the alcohol pusher in this twosome!) I'm really the only one he's confided in about his periodic concerns about his drinking. And he still drinks, not least because — in his words — most people in his life would be surprised and confused if he stopped.

A year or so ago he called to tell me about his friend from high school, whose husband was "a really bad alcoholic" who'd recently disappeared again, leaving her and the kids to worry and wonder, until he turned up in Atlantic City at the end of a days-long bender. My friend went on to tell me how abhorrent he found his guy's behavior and how bad he felt for his friend and the kids.

I listened, and I get it. It *is* awful. But what jarred me as we talked was how clearly a line had been drawn between my friend and the drunken guy "over there." Even though both men regularly drank the same stuff that sparked this guy's bender. Yet it was as if somewhere along the line, this other guy had crossed a moral threshold and was now choosing to be a loser, derelict asshole who abused his family by choosing to drink again.

The truth is, this guy probably lost his ability to choose whether or not to drink a long time ago — just like I lost mine at a certain point. But up until then, and maybe for many, many years or decades, this guy probably drank just like my friend does. I know for a fact they used to drink together, often.

My friend has admitted to me that he has no "off switch" after a few beers. Sometimes, he'll go out to dinner and only have a beer, but usually he drinks a lot more. He's suffered a lot of obvious and not-so-obvious consequences because of his drinking, and, suffice to say, his life isn't looking so great right now. Is it because of alcohol? Maybe. Is alcohol helping him out? Definitely not.

Does he see any of it this way? No. He's still over there

comparing himself to the guy who's so much worse. Which is what we all do. I certainly did.

And we compare ourselves right into a corner that's more and more difficult to crawl out of as time goes on. This comparison-based, *I'm okay because that person is worse* standard undermines the far more important question. Namely, how do you feel about your *own* drinking? Comparison is a distraction, a tool to blind ourselves from what we don't want to see. And labels like "alcoholic" support unrealistically optimistic comparisons that keep people — like me, like my friend — drinking.

I have another friend, Aidan. As she says, she doesn't have a "salacious drinking story." Rather, she calls herself a "gray-area drinker," enjoying a few glasses of wine here and there but rarely drinking too much by any standard. Her drinking certainly never appeared to be an issue to anyone else, yet drinking nagged at her for years. She would quit for periods of time and went so far as to document those occasions on her blog. Ultimately, she decided to give it up for good. Not because she labeled herself an alcoholic but because she realized her life is simply far better without it. Life without alcohol grants her greater peace of mind, less anxiety, and a generally more solid, calmer existence.

Aidan's story is so important because we don't hear examples like this. Quitting without a label is unheard of for the most part. We feel like we need a real reason to not drink, as if a clear mind, a clear heart, and a still, small voice urging us to stay present are not enough.

Am I an alcoholic? is the wrong question. It's the question we've been socialized to ask, the question I asked myself for a long time, and the question that shows up in my in-box all the time, but it's the wrong damn question.

If believing you're an alcoholic feels true, if it elevates your life by furthering you on the path to betterment and healing, believe it. If it doesn't, throw it away.

The typical question is, *Is this bad enough for me to have to change?*

The question we should be asking is, *Is this good enough for me to stay the same?*

And the real question underneath it all is, *Am I free?*

14

A Nice Little Life

There is another world, and it is in this one.

— PAUL ÉLUARD

Sara and I walked to a restaurant a few blocks from a meeting in downtown Boston. It was the first time I'd ever gone out to eat with someone from AA and definitely the first time I'd gone out to dinner without drinking in a very long time. I'd approached her a few days before and made plans to go to the meeting together and grab a bite afterward.

I'd gone to a new meeting, one I'd heard was among the bigger ones in the city, promising myself I wouldn't just run out afterward but instead would force myself to approach some-one — a woman, specifically — and try to make a connection. I'd made this promise on the heels of a work trip to New York that I drank all the way through, despite my intentions not to. I knew I had to do something else. Trying to pull off sobriety alone wasn't cutting it.

So I walked up to her after that meeting and awkwardly introduced myself. She was striking and edgy looking and appeared to be someone I might want to be friends with in real life. I started to tell her I was trying to meet women peers, that I didn't know anyone and was new and struggling — trying to build a case for what I was about to ask. But I didn't have to get very far before she asked me for my number.

It's commonplace for people to approach strangers in meetings — something that took me a long time to get used to. We exchanged a few texts that evening, and just having that single connection made me feel so much better and like I wasn't completely adrift in the world.

We went to a spot I'd been to dozens of times, a divey little place in Boston's Downtown Crossing area where I'd spent many hours drinking endless beers and martinis and glasses of wine. Jake and I had stopped there to grab a drink before going to a movie down the street on one of our first dates. I'd drank dirty martinis there with my girlfriends before going to shows at the Orpheum next door. Happy hours. Work lunches.

As we walked down the steps to the entrance, all the memories flooded back and every cell in me was screaming for a drink. I actually started to think of excuses why I had to suddenly go home — maybe Jake had called with an emergency involving Alma, or I'd forgotten a work deadline. It just felt so wrong, so unfathomable, to imagine the entire process of sitting down and having dinner and making my way through a conversation without drinking.

I stayed. We both ordered Diet Cokes with lime and some food, and luckily, she did most of the talking, probably because she sensed I was struggling. She told me some of her story, much of which was strikingly similar to mine, and that was comforting to a degree, but the whole time I felt like I was on the verge of a panic attack. I ate very little and marveled as she seemed to have command over her words and her story and to genuinely enjoy her food. I hadn't had a stomach for eating for months.

Her phone sat next to her plate, facedown, and a couple of times she checked her texts and smiled.

When we were waiting for our bill, I asked her what I wanted to know more than anything else: "Do you like your life now?"

I had suspected, even after hearing enough stories of how grateful people were, how different their lives had become — even after hearing Kacey tell me hundreds of times how much she loved her life in sobriety — that they were all faking it a little, or a lot. I believed that they'd grown to accept their life but not to really *love* it, and that deep down they were all fundamentally dissatisfied but wouldn't admit it, not even to themselves.

She straightened her napkin on her lap, then looked up at me. "I have a nice little life," she said.

I nodded, hoping for more.

"I have at least fifteen people in here who I can call anytime, and count on," she said, as she laid her palm over her phone. "I never had that before."

The part about the people was nice, but my heart sank, because I thought her words confirmed what I imagined: sobriety was less-than. Boring. A *B* version of life that nobody *really* wanted. She had learned to live with it — but it wasn't the dream. ·

I had never wanted "a nice little life." I wanted a big, vast, expansive, exciting one. I had so many things I wanted to do and see and experience, and I thought sobriety meant cutting much of that off.

For a while, as I've told you, things *did* get smaller. Out of necessity, I had to pull back from a lot of people in my life and most of the things I used to do, just so I could give myself a shot. Energetically, I had the capacity for so much less. I tried to focus on simple, basic routines — a small list of nonnegotiables that kept me steady and safe enough — and doing so was just about all I could manage.

Besides, I had a hard time finding any rest or joy in much of anything. While other people seemed to be content going to movies, or learning to knit, or going out to dinner with other sober people, for me almost everything felt blanched and flat.

There were a few exceptions. For one, words seemed to want to pour out of me. I would wake in the middle of the night and have an intense urge to write something down or to try to answer a question I'd heard someone ask at a meeting or work out something on my mind. I'd go to my kitchen and furiously type or scribble in one of my notebooks until I was emptied and then go back to bed for an hour before getting Alma up and going to work.

I kept a running list of essay or blog-post ideas in my Notes app on my phone, and I'd continually add to it, review it, edit it. At work, I'd often shut myself in a conference room and dump all my thoughts into a document so I'd have the space to focus on work again. Sometimes I shared these things on my blog. Other times I just kept the files on my computer.

I recently found a document with over twenty-five thousand words from that time — small essays and descriptions of things I was experiencing — that I don't even remember writing. Just to give you some perspective: that's *half a book*. So while I thought my life was "small and boring," something significant and marvelous was growing at the same time — something born straight from sobriety.

I also experienced occasional bursts of visceral energy, like waves rolling through me, that compelled me to physically move my body in order to withstand them. This wasn't new. It was the "big energy" I mentioned in the introduction.

It was often an overwhelming and scary feeling, like drinking too much coffee or falling in love, and it was this upper register of things that felt so hard to explain. I think one of the things I was doing with drinking was trying to bring down this energy so I could survive it. Alcohol was a very effective way to slow down that frequency, and the raucousness of partying was a way to stop it completely.

In this way, drinking felt useful, and even necessary. But in those early months of sobriety, when these waves hit, I ran and I ran and I ran instead of drinking, pounding my feet to the ground for as long as I could stand. On my runs, that manic frequency could be metabolized and channeled, and as my body moved and my breath deepened, the raw, unfocused energy transformed into a hot anger or a potent conviction or something else useful. And then, because I wasn't incapacitated by the cycle of drinking or recovering from drinking, I could actually take steps to turn my thoughts and ideas into something — either by writing, creating a new workshop, making connections, reading something, starting a project with Alma, or having a real conversation.

It was as if, all those years, I had been stopping some primal cycle halfway through. I had been *almost* feeling, *almost* doing, *almost* living, all the while believing I was going full-out. Drinking hadn't made anything bigger, or better, or *more*. Drinking was the stop. It was the obstacle to my Big Life.

In my late-twenties and thirties, I had associated the responsibilities of adult life and motherhood with smallness and tedium. Drinking was an antidote to that, I believed. It added color. Fun. A way to reject the more traditional doctrines of my role as a woman, a mother, a wife, a successful businessperson. It was something that was *mine*, and with my friends and other moms, it was *ours* — our little symbol of sovereignty and independence, when it felt like the identities we had established earlier in life were bleeding into our kids and jobs and whatever else we were trying to manage.

It was proof, if only to myself, that I was still young, subversive, and not going to succumb to the monotony of a normal, suburban existence.

What this looked like in reality was a lot of shiny exterior and zero stability underneath. Yes, I had the fancy title and traveled to places like Hong Kong for work, but I couldn't even get approved for a credit card. I lived in a lovely home with an outstanding view of the water, but the rent was well beyond what I could afford, and inside, there were piles of boxes still unpacked from four moves ago and unfinished projects everywhere. I met all kinds of men and had salacious stories to entertain my married friends or people at work, but I felt empty and desperate about it most of the time. I made six figures, but my phone still got turned off regularly because I forgot to pay my bill. Most nights I fell asleep without even brushing my teeth.

Little by little, as I accumulated more sobriety, I started to tend to the basic tasks of daily life. Putting groceries in the fridge and toilet paper in the bathroom. Washing my face. Folding laundry. Drinking a cool glass of water in the morning, without the four-Advil chaser. Making coffee at home, with fresh half-and-half. Emptying the trash out of my car. Filling it with gas before it started sputtering. Opening my mail. Checking my bank account balance. Paying a parking ticket on time. Making my bed. Planning playdates for Alma. Renewing my driver's license. Replacing a broken lightbulb.

These things — these small, simple things that I had long ignored, never learned how to do, or just assumed would magically happen as a passive by-product of getting older — they were not small at all. They were the necessary building blocks of the life I had been living. Except I had never really owned them. I had never really *owned* my life.

Each little step I took to make something mine, every time I owned some small aspect of my world, took care and tended to it, I felt an almost shocking sense of pride. So much of this part was quiet, internal, and went largely unnoticed day after day. Nobody was sending congratulations cards for changing the lightbulb. These weren't things anyone would post on Instagram or gush to friends about.

It wasn't the stuff of a big, splashy life, as I had long envisioned it, but rather a slow, steady march toward something so much more substantial: I was finally growing up.

My friend Kate once quipped about my emotionality by saying that "my rainbow is very bright." Meaning, I feel things big and bright. And while this is certainly true, as time went on in my drinking, my emotional range began to narrow, and my displays of emotion became erratic. I thought drinking brought me into more depth, but it was an artificial amplification of only a few emotions. Instead I started to have the sense that I was *supposed* to feel certain things in certain situations, but I couldn't actually access those emotions, only facsimiles of them. I knew I wanted to feel more connected to my daughter, for example — I could sense my adoration for her; it was right there underneath a gauzy numbness. But most things, including her, honestly felt "in the way" and secondary to the draw of my next glass of wine.

I wanted to feel genuinely happy for my friends when something wonderful happened to them, or to find that blanketed peace of getting lost in a movie or a book plot, or to feel the simple joy in a meandering conversation, or to remember what had felt so pure and clear about my relationship with Jake at one time, or to even feel enough sadness that I might cry spontaneously, without the help of a bottle of wine. But over time I only felt a few things in extremes — anxiety, shame, and occasionally excitement — and I mistook the vicissitudes for emotional depth.

As I started to thaw out in sobriety, my emotions resurfaced and filled out again. At first, I felt attacked by them — the saying goes that feelings start "coming out of you sideways" when you sober up. It was a lot like riding a roller coaster for a while: up, down, up — up — up, *dramatic* drop, with no warning or logic. But eventually, things evened out and I started to look at my emotions as messengers, energies that existed to inform me of something or get me to pay attention.

Today, I am astonished by the immediacy of my delight and the readiness of my tears. I used to go months and even years without crying; now, it happens spontaneously when something strikes me as moving, sad, or even beautiful — especially that. I howl with laughter. I feel joy for no reason. Snuggling up to my daughter at night, closing another day with a clear conscience, fills me with a gratitude too thick for words.

Grief can pull me swiftly into its river. It's fascinating to think back on my conversation with Sara — to consider the narrow emotional band in which I was operating then — and to marvel that I thought I had anything to lose. I had lost so much already, and even more important, I had barely scratched the surface on the infinite aliveness inside me.

It is counterintuitive that restriction might offer expansiveness. By and large, we believe more is better. Thirty-one flavors of ice cream instead of three. Eighteen different types of shampoo. Three hundred eighty-five channels on TV and fifteen ways to order a coffee. My years in sobriety have proved the opposite to be true. The years have been a continual process of letting go, layer by layer, of what would appear to many — and what I would have always considered — to be a largeness. A bounty of choice. Freedom.

At first, and for a long while, it was just the drinking. It took all I had to let that go — to simply not drink, day after day. In the second year, it became about emotional sobriety, which — although it has many dimensions — could be boiled down to learning to hear and speak the truth. Relationships that no longer fit who I was becoming naturally fell away.

Eventually, I started to look at money and my finances and to get clean around that. This was as simple as understanding for the first time exactly how much debt I had: to actually write down the number. And then, to wrap my head around that number in a concrete way, as something to be owned and managed and tackled, instead of the nebulous blob of heaviness I assumed would somehow evaporate or simply be part of me, like an organ, until I died.

In 2016, less than two years into sobriety, I listened to the small voice that had been whispering inside me for so long — to that pulse of "big energy" I told you about — and leaped into work much closer to my heart. (And this was only possible because I had been consistently *acting on* what for years I had only talked about: namely, writing.)

In year three, I moved into (and could actually afford renting) a place that was exactly, *exactly* what I wanted: small, quaint, and so close to the water that I can taste the salt in the air. When I moved, I sold just about everything I owned: all the old furniture from my marriage, the collection of hand-me-down and Craigslist belongings I'd been carting around since my twenties, a rug I bought because it was cheap but hated, and a whole assortment of other items I had accumulated but didn't identify with at all.

My whole adult life I'd considered myself incapable of pulling together a cohesively designed room. I would stand in the aisles of a store and be overcome with paralysis at the choices, and inevitably I'd choose things I would later hate. But suddenly, I knew precisely what I wanted. The colors, the textures, the lines, and the aesthetic came to me clear as day. I went from places decorated in heavy, dark colors — browns, reds, blacks, a spray of random accents — to a simple palette of gray, dusty pink, cornflower blue, and white, so much white. It was me. I can't tell you how satisfying it was to stand back and see my home and realize: *This is me. It is mine. I did it.*

Before I moved, I set up tarps in the living room of my old apartment, and any furniture I wanted to keep I painted white. I bought lamps and simple wall hangings, donated old art pieces, reframed photos, and printed new ones. Within a couple of weeks, I chose the perfect gray couch, a gray-and-white marble coffee table, gorgeous handwoven rugs, modern white Scandinavian-style pieces for my living room and bedroom.

I designed Alma's bedroom with her: mermaid theme, a proper dresser, a grown-up bed, and ocean-themed artwork. The decisions were intentional, simple, and so easy. And when I moved into my new place, I saw that my surroundings — for the first time in my adult life — finally mirrored the heart I could now trust as bright, resplendent, calm, and most of all, clear.

In year four, I finally stopped taking Ambien, a medication I was prescribed before Alma was born to battle insomnia. Although I had always obtained the medication legally and didn't take more than the prescribed dose of 10 mg, I also never, ever went without it in those ten years, save a few random stretches. I told myself my use of it was necessary and fine, but I also knew — the way we always know when we are up to something — that I relied too heavily on it. I thought about that stupid pill all the time: it was my fire door, a guaranteed brief period of escape at the end of the day, no matter what. As the years ticked on in sobriety, it haunted me more and more, because I had the sense that that *little* prescribed pill allowed me to get just a *little* drunk every night.

Eventually, in late spring of 2018, I became excessively tired. Listless. Almost depressed. Winter was coming to a close, and I couldn't blame it on the cold darkness any longer. When I woke up in the morning and had that same metallic taste in my mouth — a marker of having taken the medication — I felt dirty. Disappointed. Like a big fraud. Occasionally, I would wake to see a response to a text I didn't remember sending, or an empty bowl with a spoon in it on my bedside table and I'd struggle to recall what I ate.

It was haunting — way too much like the past.

At the time, I was working with my agent to sell this book. And I had a pit of knowing in my belly that if I didn't quit, I would never sell it — and would certainly never be able to finish writing it if it did sell, either. I spoke to my doctor, and she told me she didn't see any problem with the dose I was taking, which was what every doctor prior had told me as well. But I *knew*. I knew it was time.

I prepared myself as much as I could by learning about the negative effects of the medication, meditating, and creating the best possible sleep environment for myself. Then I stumbled upon Matthew Walker's eye-opening book *Why We Sleep* and discussed with a friend, for the first time ever, what I had been doing. Then, finally, I took the leap.

It took a little bit of time to recalibrate my sleeping. I was afraid and raw again. But soon enough, I was sleeping through the night. I was remembering my dreams. And I was waking up with the same sense of disbelief and gratitude that had accompanied my first days of sobriety. I was free of another thing that had owned part of me. *Again.* And sure enough, after quitting Ambien, I was able to write several chapters of this book in quick succession, and it sold soon thereafter.

Over all these years, piece by piece, I also started to repair my relationship to men. As I've said, this will continue to be the work of my life, but I have come from a place of feeling completely out of control — triggered all the time, reacting, and grasping — to one of growing dignity and self-worth. I still have the voice of an old therapist in my mind, who said, quite matter-of-factly, "You will probably always struggle to have a healthy relationship with a man," and when I think of that, I want to break things.

But then I think, *So what? So what if I do?*

Recently, I went on a date with a man I met on Bumble (dear God, I might have to write a book about the special animal that is dating online, and dating in your forties, next). We matched and, within an hour, decided to meet up for "a drink," per his suggestion.

I didn't clarify beforehand that I didn't drink alcohol because I didn't need to. In the early years, this would have been a rub for me — I would have wanted him to know in advance to alleviate my own anxiety and also so there would be no escape hatch, even figuratively, for me to choose otherwise.

I chose the place, a place significantly closer to me than him, because I didn't mind asking him to drive a distance to meet me. I arrived early and picked the table I wanted. And when he arrived, it was clear we both found the other attractive. We talked. We flirted. He drank a first, second, and then third glass of wine without noticing that I was sipping fizzy water.

I eventually ordered some food, and while we were sharing oysters, I realized — while watching him add a tiny scoop of mignonette to the salty, watery thing — that in the past, certainly while drinking but even in the earlier years of sobriety, it would have been inevitable that the date would have gone on longer into the night. I would have overlooked things about him that were passable to me but not entirely attractive, just to disappear into something for a while or to feel awash in attention. I would have given him premature access to my energy and my body. I would have overlooked the fact that I really didn't like that he guzzled three large goblets of wine in a matter of ninety minutes, because I would have been trying to prove to myself or to him that I was *so cool with all of it.*

In hundreds of conscious and unconscious ways, I would have bypassed my own intuition, preferences, and desires, in order to feel wanted.

At some undefinable moment, I knew the date was done. I knew I would go home alone, to my clean bed in my haven of a home with my two kitties and have a sweet night of sleep. I would wake up fresh, regretting nothing, and — most of all — knowing I gave absolutely nothing away for the wrong reasons.

Most recently, I started to pay attention to something I had been stubbornly and willfully ignoring since I got sober: my diet. From my history with eating disorders and an extreme aversion to anything that looks like too much structure in terms of what I eat, I had forcibly pushed away any hint of restriction while also becoming increasingly aware that my sugar habit was...well, *excessive.* I didn't care until I cared, and then suddenly it felt the same way the Ambien did to me: I cared a lot and was ready to look at it. So I spent the next few months cleaning up what I put in my body, and that, too, has been transformative.

I wanted to lay all these phases out for you because first of all, it takes *time.*

But also, I know if you are facing giving up anything you cannot imagine living without, and especially if you are facing sobriety, you cannot imagine that a life exists on the other side that you'd actually want to live. And even if you are years into sobriety, you might be asking yourself if this is all there is.

Sometimes people new to sobriety tell me they feel so completely overwhelmed by the mess they have to clean up or the work they need to do. They don't know where to begin or how to prioritize. I tell them they don't have to plot it out. Life will present itself to them. One thing you can count on is that there will never be any shortage of opportunities for growth. You don't need to go out searching for ways to become enlightened; just go sit in traffic, or spend a few days with your family, and you'll find more than a treasure's worth of material.

You only need to do the next thing in front of you. Be willing and open to receiving the assignments that come organically through the people and tasks of your daily life. Extend the horizon of your timeline for improvement out about ten years longer than where you have it set now.

And know this: each step contains joy, if you decide to notice it. Even in the most difficult stretches of these years, I have been humbled just to be here at all. In this way, sobriety has forever changed my baseline: everything difficult is relative to the living hell I once inhabited, so nothing is really that difficult. And everything good is a miracle.

How wrong I had been in my understanding of Sara's words. How wrong I had been in my understanding of nearly everything that makes this life worth living. I understood her expression *a nice little life* to mean a paltry, pale existence. I didn't know the difference between the cheap, thin drama of a drinking life and the rich, layered texture of a sober one. Which is to say an *awake* one. I mistook the limited expression of outer life for the unlimited expanse of the inner one. I didn't see — couldn't possibly have seen — all that would come forth from simply allowing space to exist.

I didn't know that I would discover the diamond in the

center of my chest — the solid, indestructible, perfect place from which everything else radiates outward.

Rainer Maria Rilke's fine words have come to me time and again in this journey through sobriety:

I live my life in widening circles
that reach out across the world.

Yes, this is precisely how it's been. And how it continues to be.

I sometimes touch it physically, my chest. I press the pads of my fingers into the space, just to the right of my heart, where my ribs fuse together. The place where I imagine the diamond to be. Spontaneously, in meditation, or at the end of teaching a class, or when I've just read a line of poetry or prayer that moves me, or when I wake to another day and remember I am no longer afraid of myself, I touch it. And I sway.

Back and forth, back and forth, back and forth.

You can try this right now. You might be able to feel it, too.

That you are part of something.

You are part of this life, and it *wants* — it wants more than anything — for you to answer its call.

Diamonds are made from heat and pressure. The mistakes and pain and terror can make your bones strong for you, if you allow them to. Mine shaped me. They showed me — pushed me so hard up against — the edges of myself and forced me to answer the question *What do you want, sweet girl? What do you really, really want?*

And I found it was this.

It has always been this.

To have a direct experience of life. To know its depths

completely. To be enraptured in the mystery. To be the hero of my own great adventure.

This is the full stanza of Rilke's poem, "Widening Circles":

> I live my life in widening circles
> that reach out across the world.
> I may not complete this last one
> but I give myself to it.

Later he reveals that what he's circling around is God itself. "The primordial tower," he calls it. And this is the best way I can describe the unfurling of sobriety: a giving to, a giving in, a learning to dance with the Divine. Slowly, messily, and to my utter and surprising relief, what I've found as I go along is this: less me and more God.

It is a nice little life. It is bigger than I ever imagined.

Acknowledgments

I used to read acknowledgments in books and marvel at the number of people the author listed. It made the work seem unimaginably large and complicated. Turns out, it is. It is a bit like getting sober: if someone told you what you were in for, you probably wouldn't do it (*smile*).

But I would. I would do both things all over again. One thousand times.

Writing this book has been at once humbling, exciting, dreadful, and a blast. Mostly, I just can't believe I get to be here. What a privilege.

Huge thanks to my agent, Alexander Field, for your belief in me and your steadfastness. For answering my amateur questions, for assuring me that this book would find a home, and for being an overall champion of me and my work. Thank you to Ally Fallon for taking me on, as neurotic as I was at the time I found you, and using your magic to help shape my story. Thank you to the team at New World Library for taking a chance on me, and to my kind and wise editor, Jason Gardner, for making this book come to life.

This story wouldn't have happened without a lot of pain. And much of that pain was not mine. To the people who walked with me and watched me and carried me and stood by when all I did was take: I am humbly, eternally grateful.

Dad, Mom and Derek, Joe and Jenny, Shane, and baby Gavin: With the exception of the babies, thank God, you all have had to clean up more than a few messes and then stand by and hope that I stayed afloat. I can't imagine the terror in that. I love you. I hope to spend the rest of my life *not* scaring you.

To Lucille and Paul, and the rest of the G & S families, for continuing to care for me and treat me like family. Big Paul, I am really sorry I drank all your expensive beer that time.

To Kate Carlson, for loving me through the best and worst of it and being patient when you didn't have to be and for sharing half of our lives' worth of history together. That, I have learned, is its own great gift.

To Meadow DeVor, for being awkward at showing that you love me and for understanding that's how much I love you, too, and for being my favorite 3-7/single-mama/mama-of-a-daughter combo. Would I exist today without our FaceTime calls, your listening, your talking, your sharing, your continual refrains of "I know" and "Me too"? I'm not sure I would.

To Brooke Mays, for showing up right on time, being the best 2 in all the land, holding it all up behind the scenes, and having the most excellent GIF arsenal and sense of humor.

To Becky Vollmer, for being the best cheerleader and sister. You are proof that God works through the internet.

To Holly Whitaker — I mean, where the hell do I even start? We held hands and jumped off a cliff into a world that only we could build together, and we had to build it as we were falling. I am so proud of you. I am so proud of us.

To Jon, for being a crazy-maker but also my biggest fan from day one. You made it into the book! (You were always going to make it into the book.)

To Elena Brower, for being the first one to hear the last paragraphs of this book, for listening across the line in Australia, for crying with me and saying, "Yes, yes, that is the ending." How lucky I am to cross your path in this life.

To my Marblehead crew, for putting up with hearing me talk about this book for the past hundred years, for making me feel like I have a home again, for being Framily, for all the card playing and the skiing and the beach days and the raising kids together, I love you all a whole heck of a lot.

To the girls in Monterey, who helped me learn to stay; to all the people in the rooms who showed me what it means to show up, especially to Kristen, Tara, Kenny, and Andy, for scooping me up and carrying me along; to Jim T. and Jim Z. (and family!), for our work sessions and talks and laughs, and for making my life brighter and better; to Veronica, for saving my life in year three; to Sarah Hepola, for saying just the right things over text to keep me afloat when I was depressed and just sure I couldn't finish this book; to Jenny, who was the first landing spot and my way in; and to Grant, for telling me it would get better, then worse, then different. You were right.

To my teachers: Ann Dowsett, Elena Brower, Meggan Watterson, Dani Shapiro, and so many others who helped me believe I could do this — that it was worth doing.

To Alma's dad, for showing me what a steady love can look like and, above all, for being the father you are to her. She will never have to question where the ground is.

And to Alma, more than anyone or anything, forever. You make it all so worth it.

Permission
Acknowledgments

About the Author

Laura McKowen had a successful career in public relations and the *Mad Men*–esque drinking culture of advertising. After getting sober, she quickly became recognized as a fresh voice in recovery, beloved for her soulful and irreverent writing online and in print. She now leads sold-out retreats and courses, teaching people how to say yes to a bigger life.

Laura writes an award-winning blog, hosted the iTunes Top 100 *HOME* podcast, and has been featured by the *Guardian*, *WebMD*, the *New York Post*, Bravo, the *Today* show, and more. Laura has an MBA from Babson College and spent fifteen years in advertising, managing million-dollar accounts for Fortune 100 companies, before transitioning to writing and teaching. She's the founder of several online programs for sobriety, personal development, and writing and teaches workshops and retreats all over the United States. Laura lives outside Boston, Massachusetts, with her daughter. *We Are the Luckiest* is her first book.

www.lauramckowen.com